THE BOOK OF LIES

Jabberwoke Pocket Occult Collection

~

Crystal Gazing by Frater Achad

Heavenly Bridegrooms by Ida Craddock

Moonchild by Aleister Crowley

The Kybalion by Three Initiates

The So-Called Occult by Carl Jung

The Great God Pan by Arthur Machen

The Witch Cult by Margaret Murray

The Book of Lies by Frater Perdurabo

A Midsommar Night's Dream by William Shakespeare

Satan: A Novel by Mark Twain

~

LIBER CCCXXXIII

THE BOOK OF LIES

WHICH IS ALSO FALSELY CALLED

BREAKS

THE WANDERINGS OR FALSIFICATIONS OF THE ONE THOUGHT

OF

FRATER PERDURABO

WHICH THOUGHT IS ITSELF UNTRUE

" Break, break, break
　At the foot of thy stones, O Sea !
And I would that I could utter
　The thoughts that arise in me !"

SAN FRANSISCO : JABBERWOKE
2021

THE BOOK OF LIES Copyright © 1912 by Frater Perdurabo.

COMMENTARIES Copyright © 1923 by Aleister Crowley.

POCKET OCCULT EDITION Copyright © 2021 by Jabberwoke.

All rights reserved.

Printed in the USA.

First Jabberwoke Paperback Edition: September 2021.

Cover Photographs by Laylah Waddell, the Scarlet Woman.

Designed by S.R.L.

Paperback ISBN: 978-1-954873-37-7

10 9 8 7 6 5 4 3 2 1

FalselyCalledBreaks.com

LIBER CCCXXXIII

A∴ A∴ PUBLICATION IN CLASSES
C AND D

OFFICIAL FOR BABES OF THE ABYSS

IMPRIMATUR.

N.

Fra∴ A∴ A∴

THE BOOK OF LIES

WHICH IS ALSO FALSELY
CALLED

BREAKS

ΚΕΦΑΛΗ Η ΟΥΚ ΕΣΤΙ ΚΕΦΑΛΗ

O ! [1]

THE ANTE PRIMAL TRIAD WHICH IS NOT-GOD

> Nothing is.
> Nothing Becomes.
> Nothing is not.

THE FIRST TRIAD WHICH IS GOD
I AM.
> I utter The Word.
> I hear The Word.

THE ABYSS
The Word is broken up.
There is Knowledge.
Knowledge is Relation.
These fragments are Creation.
The broken manifests Light.[2]

o

THE SECOND TRIAD WHICH IS GOD

GOD the Father and Mother is concealed in Generation.

GOD is concealed in the whirling energy of Nature.

GOD is manifest in gathering : harmony : consideration : the Mirror of the Sun and of the Heart.

THE THIRD TRIAD

Bearing : preparing.
Wavering : flowing : flashing.
Stability : begetting.

THE TENTH EMANATION

The world.

ΚΕΦΑΛΗ Α

I

THE SABBATH OF THE GOAT

O ! the heart of N.O.X. the Night of Pan.
ΠΑΝ : Duality : Energy : Death.
Death : Begetting : the supporters of O !
To beget is to die ; to die is to beget.
Cast the Seed into the Field of Night.
Life and Death are two names of A.
Neither of these alone is enough.

ΚΕΦΑΛΗ Β

II

THE CRY OF THE HAWK

Hoor hath a secret fourfold name : it is Do What Thou Wilt.[3]
Four Words : Naught—One—Many—All.
    Thou—Child !
    Thy Name is holy.
    Thy Kingdom is come.
    Thy Will is done.
    Here is the Bread.
    Here is the Blood.
    Bring us through Temptation !
    Deliver us from Good and Evil !
That Mine as Thine be the Crown of the Kingdom, even now.
    ABRAHADABRA.
These ten words are four, the Name of the One.

ΚΕΦΑΛΗ Γ

III

THE OYSTER

The Brothers of A∴ A∴ are one with the Mother of the Child.[4]

The Many is as adorable to the One as the One is to the Many. This is the Love of These ; creation-parturition is the Bliss of the One ; coition-dissolution is the Bliss of the Many.

The All, thus interwoven of These, is Bliss.

Naught is beyond Bliss.

The Man delights in uniting with the Woman ; the Woman in parting from the Child.

The Brothers of A∴ A∴ are Women: the Aspirants to A∴ A∴ are Men.

ΚΕΦΑΛΗ Β

IV

PEACHES

Soft and hollow, how thou dost overcome the hard and full !

It dies, it gives itself ; to Thee is the fruit !

Be thou the Bride ; thou shalt be the Mother hereafter.

To all impressions thus. Let them not overcome thee ; yet let them breed within thee.

The least of the impressions, come to its perfection, is Pan.

Receive a thousand lovers ; thou shalt bear but One Child.

This child shall be the heir of Fate the Father.

ΚΕΦΑΛΗ Ε

V

THE BATTLE OF THE ANTS

That is not which is.
The only Word is Silence.
The only Meaning of that Word is not.
Thoughts are false.
Fatherhood is unity disguised as duality.
Peace implies war.
Power implies war.
Harmony implies war.
Victory implies war.
Glory implies war.
Foundation implies war.
Alas ! for the Kingdom wherein all these are at war.

ΚΕΦΑΛΗ F

VI

CAVIAR

The Word was uttered : the One exploded into one thousand million worlds.

Each world contained a thousand million spheres.

Each sphere contained a thousand million planes.

Each plane contained a thousand million stars

Each star contained a many thousand million things.

Of these the reasoner took six, and, preening, said : This is the One and the All.

These six the Adept harmonised, and said : This is the Heart of the One and the All.

These six were destroyed by the Master of the Temple ; and he spake not.

The Ash thereof was burnt up by the Magus into The Word.

Of all this did the Ipsissimus know Nothing.

Frater Perdurabo
in the Deosai Plateau
End of his first Himalayan Expedition.

ΚΕΦΑΛΗ Z

VII

THE DINOSAURS

None are They whose number is Six :[5] else were they six indeed.
Seven[6] are these Six that live not in the City of the Pyramids, under the Night of Pan.
There was Lao-tzŭ.
There was Siddartha.
There was Krishna.
There was Tahuti.
There was Mosheh.
There was Dionysus.[7]
There was Mahmud.
But the Seventh men called PERDURABO ; for enduring unto The End, at The End was Naught to endure.[8]
Amen.

ΚΕΦΑΛΗ Η

VIII

STEEPED HORSEHAIR

Mind is a disease of semen.
All that a man is or may be is hidden therein.
Bodily functions are parts of the machine ; silent, unless in dis-ease.
But mind, never at ease, creaketh " ' I.'
This I persisteth not, posteth not through generations, changeth momently, finally is dead.
Therefore is man only himself when lost to himself in The Charioting.

ΚΕΦΑΛΗ Θ

IX

THE BRANKS

Being is the Noun ; Form is the Adjective.
Matter is the Noun ; Motion is the Verb.
Wherefore hath Being clothed itself with Form?
Wherefore hath Matter manifested itself in Motion?
Answer not, O silent one ! For THERE is no 'wherefore', no 'because.'
The name of THAT is not known ; the Pronoun interprets, that is, misinterprets, It.
Time and Space are Adverbs.
Duality begat the Conjunction.
The Conditioned is Father of the Preposition.
The Article also marketh Division ; but the Interjection is the sound that endeth in the Silence.
Destroy therefore the Eight Parts of Speech ; the Ninth is nigh unto Truth.
This also must be destroyed before thou enterest into The Silence.
Aum.

ΚΕΦΑΛΗ Ι

X

WINDLESTRAWS

The Abyss of Hallucinations has Law and Reason ; but in Truth there is no bond between the Toys of the Gods.

This Reason and Law is the Bond of the Great Lie.

Truth ! Truth ! Truth ! crieth the Lord of the Abyss of Hallucinations.

There is no silence in that Abyss : for all that men call Silence is Its Speech.

This Abyss is also called ' Hell,' and ' The Many.' Its name is ' Consciousness,' and ' The Universe,' among men.

But THAT which neither is silent, nor speaks, rejoices therein.

ΚΕΦΑΛΗ ΙΑ

XI

THE GLOW-WORM

Concerning the Holy Three-in-Naught.
Nuit, Hadit, Ra-Hoor-Khuit, are only to be understood by the Master of the Temple.
They are above The Abyss, and contain all contradiction in themselves.
Below them is a seeming duality of Chaos and Babalon ; these are called Father and Mother, but it is not so. They are called Brother and Sister, but it is not so. They are called Husband and Wife, but it is not so.
The reflection of All is Pan : the Night of Pan is the Annihilation of the All.
Cast down through The Abyss is the Light, the Rosy Cross, the rapture of Union that destroys, that is The Way. The Rosy Cross is the Ambassador of Pan.
How infinite is the distance from This to That ! Yet All is Here and Now. Nor is there any

There or Then ; for all that is, what is it but a manifestation, that is, a part, that is, a falsehood, of THAT which is not?

Yet THAT which is not neither is nor is not That which is !

Identity is perfect ; therefore the Law of Identity is but a lie. For there is no subject, and there is no predicate ; nor is there the contradictory of either of these things.

Holy, Holy, Holy are these Truths that I utter, knowing them to be but falsehoods, broken mirrors, troubled waters ; hide me, O our Lady, in Thy Womb ! for I may not endure the rapture.

In this utterance of falsehood upon falsehood, whose contradictories are also false. it seems as if That which I uttered not were true.

Blessed, unutterably blessed, is this last of the illusions; let me play the man, and thrust it from me ! Amen.

ΚΕΦΑΛΗ ΙΒ

XII

THE DRAGON-FLIES

IO is the cry of the lower as OI of the higher.
In figures they are 1001 ;[9] in letters they are Joy.[10]
For when all is equilibrated, when all is beheld from without all, there is joy, joy, joy that is but one facet of a diamond, every other facet whereof is more joyful than joy itself.

ΚΕΦΑΛΗ ΙΓ

XIII

PILGRIM-TALK

O thou that settest out upon The Path, false is the Phantom that thou seekest. When thou hast it thou shalt know all bitterness, thy teeth fixed in the Sodom-Apple.

Thus hast thou been lured along That Path, whose terror else had driven thee far away.

O thou that stridest upon the middle of The Path, no phantoms mock thee. For the stride's sake thou stridest.

Thus art thou lured along That Path, whose fascination else had driven thee far away.

O thou that drawest toward the End of The Path, effort is no more. Faster and faster dost thou fall ; thy weariness is changed into Ineffable Rest.

For there is no Thou upon That Path : thou hast become The Way.

ΚΕΦΑΛΗ ΙΔ

XIV

ONION-PEELINGS

The Universe is the Practical Joke of the General at the Expense of the Particular, quoth FRATER PERDURABO, and laughed.

But those disciples nearest to him wept, seeing the Universal Sorrow.

Those next to them laughed, seeing the Universal Joke.

Below these certain disciples wept.

Then certain laughed.

Others next wept.

Others next laughed.

Next others wept.

Next others laughed.

Last came those that wept because they could not see the Joke, and those that laughed lest they should be thought not to see the Joke, and thought it safe to act like FRATER PERDURABO.

But though FRATER PERDURABO laughed openly, He also at the same time wept secretly; and in Himself He neither laughed nor wept.

Nor did He mean what He said.

ΚΕΦΑΛΗ ΙΕ

XV

THE GUN-BARREL

Mighty and erect is this Will of mine, this Pyramid of fire whose summit is lost in Heaven. Upon it have I burned the corpse of my desires.

Mighty and erect is this Φαλλος of my Will. The seed thereof is That which I have borne within me from Eternity ; and it is lost within the Body of Our Lady of the Stars.

I am not I ; I am but an hollow tube to bring down Fire from Heaven.

Mighty and marvellous is this Weakness, this Heaven which draweth me into Her Womb, this Dome which hideth, which absorbeth, Me.

This is The Night wherein I am lost, the Love through which I am no longer I.

ΚΕΦΑΛΗ ΙΣ

XVI

THE STAG-BEETLE

Death implies change and individuality if thou be THAT which hath no person, which is beyond the changing, even beyond changelessness, what hast thou to do with death?

The bird of individuality is ecstasy ; so also is its death.

In love the individuality is slain ; who loves not love?

Love death therefore, and long eagerly for it.

Die Daily.

ΚΕΦΑΛΗ ΙΖ

XVII

THE SWAN[11]

There is a Swan whose name is Ecstasy : it wingeth from the Deserts of the North ; it wingeth through the blue ; it wingeth over the fields of rice ; at its coming they push forth the green.

In all the Universe this Swan alone is motionless ; it seems to move, as the Sun seems to move ; such is the weakness of our sight.

O *fool*! criest thou?

Amen. Motion is relative : there is Nothing that is still.

Against this Swan I shot an arrow ; the white breast poured forth blood. Men smote me ; then, perceiving that I was but a Pure Fool, they let me pass.

Thus and not otherwise I came to the Temple of the Graal.

ΚΕΦΑΛΗ ΙΗ

XVIII

DEWDROPS

Verily, love is death, and death is life to come.

Man returneth not again ; the stream floweth not uphill ; the old life is no more ; there is a new life that is not his.

Yet that life is of his very essence ; it is more He than all that he calls He.

In the silence of a dewdrop is every tendency of his soul, and of his mind, and of his body ; it is the Quintessence and the Elixir of his being. Therein are the forces that made him and his father and his father's father before him.

This is the Dew of Immortality.

Let this go free, even as It will ; thou art not its master, but the vehicle of It.

ΚΕΦΑΛΗ ΙΘ

XIX

THE LEOPARD AND THE DEER

The spots of the leopard are the sunlight in the glade ; pursue thou the deer stealthily at thy pleasure.

The dappling of the deer is the sunlight in the glade ; concealed from the leopard do thou feed at thy pleasure.

Resemble all that surroundeth thee ; yet be Thyself—and take thy pleasure among the living.

This is that which is written—Lurk !—in The Book of The Law.

XX

SAMSON

The Universe is in equilibrium; therefore He that is without it, though his force be but a feather, can overturn the Universe.
Be not caught within that web, O child of Freedom ! Be not entangled in the universal lie, O child of Truth !

ΚΕΦΑΛΗ ΚΑ

XXI

THE BLIND WEBSTER

It is not necessary to understand : it is enough to adore.

The god may be of clay : adore him ; he becomes GOD.

We ignore what created us ; we adore what we create. Let us create nothing but GOD !

That which causes us to create is our true father and mother ; we create in our own image, which is theirs.

Let us create therefore without fear ; for we can create nothing that is not GOD.

ΚΕΦΑΛΗ ΚΒ

XXII

THE DESPOT

The waiters of the best eating-houses mock the whole world ; they estimate every client at his proper value.

This I know certainly, because they always treat me with profound respect. Thus they have flattered me into praising them thus publicly.

Yet it is true ; and they have this insight because they serve, and because they can have no personal interest in the affairs of those whom they serve.

An absolute monarch would be absolutely wise and good.

But no man is strong enough to have no interest. Therefore the best king would be Pure Chance.

It is Pure Chance that rules the Universe ; therefore, and only therefore, life is good.

ΚΕΦΑΛΗ ΚΓ

XXIII

SKIDOO

What man is at ease in his Inn?
Get out.
Wide is the world and cold.
Get out.
Thou hast become an in-itiate.
Get out.
But thou canst not get out by the way thou camest in. The Way out is THE WAY.
Get out.
For OUT is Love and Wisdom and Power.[12]
Get OUT.
If thou hast T already, first get UT.[13]
Then get O.
And so at last get OUT.

XXIV

THE HAWK AND THE BLINDWORM

This book would translate Beyond-Reason into the words of Reason.

Explain thou snow to them of Andaman.

The slaves of reason call this book Abuse-of-Language : they are right.

Language was made for men to eat and drink, make love, do barter, die. The wealth of a language consists in its Abstracts ; the poorest tongues have wealth of Concretes.

Therefore have Adepts praised silence ; at least it does not mislead as speech does.

Also, Speech is a symptom of Thought.

Yet, silence is but the negative side of Truth ; the positive side is beyond even silence.

Nevertheless, One True God crieth *hriliu !* And the laughter of the Death-rattle is akin.

ΚΕΦΑΛΗ ΚΕ

XXV

THE STAR RUBY

Facing East, in the centre, draw deep deep deep thy breath, closing thy mouth with thy right forefinger prest against thy lower lip. Then dashing down the hand with a great sweep back and out, expelling forcibly thy breath, cry : ΑΠΟ ΠΑΝΤΟΣ ΚΑΚΟΔΑΙΜΟΝΟΣ.

With the same forefinger touch thy forehead and say ΣΟΙ, thy member, and say ΩΦΑΛΛΕ,[14] thy right shoulder, and say ΙΣΧΥΡΟΣ, thy left shoulder, and say ΕΥΧΑΡΙΣΤΟΣ ; then clasp thine hands, locking the fingers, and cry ΙΑΩ.

Advance to the East. Imagine strongly a Pentagram, aright, in thy forehead. Drawing the hands to the eyes, fling it forth, making the sign of Horus, and roar ΧΑΟΣ. Retire thine hand in the sign of Hoor pa kraat.

Go round to the North and repeat ; but scream ΒΑΒΑΛΟΝ.

Go round to the West and repeat ; but say ΕΡΩC.

Go round to the South and repeat ; but bellow ΨΥΧΗ.

Completing the circle widdershins, retire to the centre, and raise thy voice in the Paian, with these words ΙΟ ΠΑΝ with the signs of N. O. X.

Extend the arms in the form of a Tau, and say low but clear : ΠΡΟ ΜΟΥ ΙΥΓΓΕC ΟΠΙCΩ ΜΟΥ ΤΕΛΕΤΑΡΧΑΙ ΕΠΙ ΔΕΞΙΑ CΥΝΟΧΕC ΕΠΑΡΙCΤΕΡΑ ΔΑΙΜΟΝΕC ΦΛΕΓΕΙ ΓΑΡ ΠΕΡΙ ΜΟΥ Ο ΑCΤΗΡ ΤΩΝ ΠΕΝΤΕ ΚΑΙ ΕΝ ΤΗΙ CΤΗΛΗΙ Ο ΑCΤΗΡ ΤΩΝ ΕΞ ΕCΤΗΚΕ.

Repeat the Cross Qabalistic, as above, and end as thou didst begin.

ΚΕΦΑΛΗ ΚϜ

XXVI

THE ELEPHANT AND THE TORTOISE

The Absolute and the Conditioned together make The One Absolute.

The Second, who is the Fourth, the Demiurge, whom all nations of Men call The First, is a lie grafted upon a lie, a lie multiplied by a lie.

Fourfold is He, the Elephant upon whom the Universe is poised : but the carapace of the Tortoise supports and covers all.

This Tortoise is sixfold, the Holy Hexagram.[15]

These six and four are ten, 10, the One manifested that returns into the Naught unmanifest.

The All-Mighty, the All-Ruler, the All-Knower, the All-Father, adored by all men and by me abhorred, be thou accursed, be thou abolished, be thou annihilated, Amen !

ΚΕΦΑΛΗ ΚΖ

XXVII

THE SORCERER

A Sorcerer by the power of his magick had subdued all things to himself.
Would he travel? He could fly through space more swiftly than the stars.
Would he eat, drink, and take his pleasure? There was none that did not instantly obey his bidding.
In the whole system of ten million times ten million spheres upon the two and twenty million planes he had his desire.
And with all this he was but himself.
Alas !

ΚΕΦΑΛΗ ΚΗ

XXVIII

THE POLE-STAR

Love is all virtue, since the pleasure of love is but love, and the pain of love is but love.

Love taketh no heed of that which is not and of that which is.

Absence exalteth love, and presence exalteth love.

Love moveth ever from height to height of ecstasy and faileth never.

The wings of love droop not with time, nor slacken for life or for death.

Love destroyeth self, uniting self with that which is not-self, so that Love breedeth All and None in One.

Is it not so? . . . No? . . .

Then thou art not lost in love ; speak not of love.

Love Alway Yieldeth : Love Alway Hardeneth.

. . . . May be : I write it but to write Her name.

ΚΕΦΑΛΗ ΚΘ

XXIX

THE SOUTHERN CROSS

Love, I love you ! Night, night, cover us ! Thou art night, O my love : and there are no stars but thine eyes.

Dark night, sweet night, so warm and yet so fresh, so scented yet so holy, cover me, cover me !

Let me be no more ! Let me be Thine ; let me be Thou; let me be neither Thou nor I; let there be love in night and night in love.

N. O. X. the night of Pan ; and Laylah, the night before His threshold !

ΚΕΦΑΛΗ Λ

XXX

JOHN-A-DREAMS

Dreams are imperfections of sleep ; even so is consciousness the imperfection of waking.

Dreams are impurities in the circulation of the blood ; even so is consciousness a disorder of life.

Dreams are without proportion, without good sense, without truth ; so also is consciousness.

Awake from dream, the truth is known :[16] awake from waking, the Truth is—The Unknown.

ΚΕΦΑΛΗ ΛΑ

XXXI

THE GAROTTE

IT moves from motion into rest, and rests from rest into motion. These IT does alway, for time is not. So that IT does neither of these things. IT does THAT one thing which we must express by two things neither of which possesses any rational meaning.

Yet ITS doing, which is no-doing, is simple and yet complex, is neither free nor necessary.

For all these ideas express Relation ; and IT, comprehending all Relation in ITS simplicity, is out of all Relation even with ITSELF.

All this is true and false ; and it is true and false to say that it is true and false.

Strain forth thine Intelligence, O man, O worthy one, O chosen of IT, to apprehend the discourse of THE MASTER ; for thus thy reason shall at last break down, as the fetter is struck from a slave's throat.

ΚΕΦΑΛΗ ΛΒ

XXXII

THE MOUNTAINEER

Consciousness is a symptom of disease.
All that moves well moves without will.
All skillfulness, all strain, all intention is contrary to ease.

Practise a thousand times, and it becomes difficult ; a thousand thousand, and it becomes easy ; a thousand thousand times a thousand thousand, and it is no longer Thou that doeth it, but It that doeth itself through thee. Not until then is that which is done well done.

Thus spoke FRATER PERDURABO as he leapt from rock to rock of the moraine without ever casting his eyes upon the ground.

ΚΕΦΑΛΗ ΛΓ

XXXIII

BAPHOMET

A black two-headed Eagle is GOD ; even a Black Triangle is He. In His claws He beareth a sword ; yea, a sharp sword is held therein.

This Eagle is burnt up in the Great Fire ; yet not a feather is scorched. This Eagle is swallowed up in the Great Sea ; yet not a feather is wetted. So flieth He in the air, and lighteth upon the earth at His pleasure.

So spake IACOBUS BURGUNDUS MOLENSIS[17] the Grand Master of the Temple ; and of the GOD that is Ass-headed did he dare not speak.

ΚΕΦΑΛΗ ΛΔ

XXXIV

THE SMOKING DOG[18]

Each act of man is the twist and double of an hare.

Love and death are the greyhounds that course him.

God bred the hounds and taketh His pleasure in the sport.

This is the Comedy of Pan, that man should think he hunteth, while those hounds hunt him.

This is the Tragedy of Man when facing Love and Death he turns to bay. He is no more hare, but boar.

There are no other comedies or tragedies.

Cease then to be the mockery of God ; in savagery of love and death live thou and die!

Thus shall His laughter be thrilled through with Ecstasy.

ΚΕΦΑΛΗ ΛΕ

XXXV

VENUS OF MILO

Life is as ugly and necessary as the male body.

Death is as beautiful and necessary as the female body.

The soul is beyond male and female as it is beyond Life and Death.

Even as the Lingam and the Yoni are but diverse developments of One Organ, so also are Life and Death but two phases of One State. So also the Absolute and the Conditioned are but forms of THAT.

What do I love? There is no form, no being, to which I do not give myself wholly up.

Take me, who will !

ΚΕΦΑΛΗ ΛΣ

XXXVI

THE STAR SAPPHIRE

Let the Adept be armed with his Magick Rood [and provided with his Mystic Rose].

In the centre, let him give the L. V. X. signs; or if he know them, if he will and dare do them, and can keep silent about them, the signs of N. O. X. being the signs of Puer, Vir, Puella, Mulier. Omit the sign I. R.

Then let him advance to the East, and make the Holy Hexagram, saying : PATER ET MATER UNIS DEUS ARARITA.

Let him go round to the South, make the Holy Hexagram, and say : MATER ET FILIUS UNUS DEUS ARARITA.

Let him go round to the West, make the Holy Hexagram, and say : FILIUS ET FILIA UNUS DEUS ARARITA.

Let him go round to the North, make the Holy Hexagram, and then say : FILIA ET PATER UNUS DEUS ARARITA.

Let him then return to the Centre, and so to The Centre of All [making the ROSY CROSS as he may know how] saying: ARARITA ARARITA ARARITA.

[In this the Signs shall be those of Set Triumphant and of Baphomet. Also shall Set appear in the Circle. Let him drink of the Sacrament and let him communicate the same.]

Then let him say: OMNIA IN DUOS: DUO IN UNUM: UNUS IN NIHIL: HAEC NEC QUATUOR NEC OMNIA NEC DUO NEC UNUS NEC NIHIL SUNT.

GLORIA PATRI ET MATRI ET FILIO ET FILIAE ET SPIRITUI SANCTO EXTERNO ET SPIRITUI SANCTO INTERNO UT ERAT EST ERIT IN SAECULA SAECULORUM SEX IN UNO PER NOMEN SEPTEM IN UNO ARARITA.

Let him then repeat the signs of L. V. X. but not the signs of N.O.X.; for it is not he that shall arise in the Sign of Isis Rejoicing.

ΚΕΦΑΛΗ ΛΖ

XXXVII

DRAGONS

Thought is the shadow of the eclipse of Luna.
Samadhi is the shadow of the eclipse of Sol.
The moon and the earth are the non-ego and
 the ego : the Sun is THAT.
Both eclipses are darkness ; both are exceed-
 ing rare ; the Universe itself is Light.

ΚΕΦΑΛΗ ΛΗ

XXXVIII

LAMBSKIN

Cowan, skidoo !
Tyle !
Swear to hele all.
This is the mystery.
Life !
Mind is the traitor.
Slay mind.
Let the corpse of mind lie unburied on the edge of the Great Sea !
Death !
This is the mystery.
Tyle !
Cowan, skidoo !

ΚΕΦΑΛΗ ΛΘ

XXXIX

THE LOOBY

Only loobies find excellence in these words.
It is thinkable that A is not-A ; to reverse this is but to revert to the normal.
Yet by forcing the brain to accept propositions of which one set is absurdity, the other truism, a new function of brain is established.
Vague and mysterious and all indefinite are the contents of this new consciousness ; yet they are somehow vital. by use they become luminous.
Unreason becomes Experience.
This lifts the leaden-footed soul to the Experience of THAT of which Reason is the blasphemy.
But without the Experience these words are the Lies of a Looby.
Yet a Looby to thee, and a Booby to me, a Balassius Ruby to GOD, may be !

ΚΕΦΑΛΗ Μ

XL

THE HIMOG[19]

A red rose absorbs all colours but red ; red is therefore the one colour that it is not.

This Law, Reason, Time, Space, all Limitation blinds us to the Truth.

All that we know of Man, Nature, God, is just that which they are not ; it is that which they throw off as repungnant.

The HIMOG is only visible insofar as He is imperfect.

Then are they all glorious who seem not to be glorious, as the HIMOG is All-glorious Within?

It may be so.

How then distinguish the inglorious and perfect HIMOG from the inglorious man of earth?

Distinguish not !

But thyself Ex-tinguish : HIMOG art thou, and HIMOG shalt thou be.

ΚΕΦΑΛΗ ΜΑ

XLI

CORN BEEF HASH[20]

In V. V. V. V. V. is the Great Work perfect.

Therefore none is that pertaineth not to V. V. V. V. V.

In any may he manifest ; yet in one hath he chosen to manifest ; and this one hath given His ring as a Seal of Authority to the Work of the A∴ A∴ through the colleagues of FRATER PERDURABO.

But this concerns themselves and their administration ; it concerneth none below the grade of Exempt Adept, and such an one only by command.

Also, since below the Abyss Reason is Lord, let men seek by experiment, and not by Questionings.

ΚΕΦΑΛΗ ΜΒ

XLII

DUST-DEVILS

In the wind of the mind arises the turbulence[21] called I.

It breaks ; down shower the barren thoughts.
All life is choked.

This desert is the Abyss wherein is the Universe. The Stars are but thistles in that waste.

Yet this desert is but one spot accursed in a world of bliss.

Now and again Travellers cross the desert ; they come from the Great Sea, and to the Great Sea they go.

As they go they spill water ; one day they will irrigate the desert, till it flower.

See ! five footprints of a Camel ! V. V. V. V. V.

ΚΕΦΑΛΗ ΜΓ

XLIII

MULBERRY TOPS

Black blood upon the altar ! and the rustle of angel wings above !

Black blood of the sweet fruit, the bruised, the violated bloom—that setteth The Wheel a-spinning in the spire.

Death is the veil of Life, and Life of Death ; for both are Gods.

This is that which is written : " A feast for Life, and a greater feast for Death !" in THE BOOK OF THE LAW.

The blood is the life of the individual : offer then blood !

ΚΕΦΑΛΗ ΜΔ

XLIV

THE MASS OF THE PHOENIX

The Magician, his breast bare, stands before an altar on which are his Burin, Bell, Thurible, and two of the Cakes of Light. In the Sign of the Enterer he reaches West across the Altar, and cries :

Hail Ra, that goest in Thy bark
Into the Caverns of the Dark !

He gives the sign of Silence, and takes the Bell, and Fire, in his hands.

East of the Altar see me stand
With Light and Musick in mine hand !

He strikes Eleven times upon the Bell 3 3 3— 5 5 5 5 5—3 3 3 and places the Fire in the Thurible.

I strike the Bell : I light the flame :
I utter the mysterious Name.
    ABRAHADABRA

He strikes Eleven times upon the Bell.

Now I begin to pray : Thou Child,
Holy Thy name and undefiled !
Thy reign is come : Thy will is done.
Here is the Bread ; here is the Blood.
Bring me through midnight to the Sun !
Save me from Evil and from Good !
That Thy one crown of all the Ten.
Even now and here be mine. AMEN.

He puts the first Cake on the Fire of the Thurible.

I burn the Incense-cake, proclaim
These adorations of Thy name.

He makes them as in Liber Legis, and strikes again Eleven times upon the Bell. With the Burin he then makes upon his breast the proper sign.

Behold this bleeding breast of mine
Gashed with the sacramental sign !

He puts the second Cake to the wound.

I stanch the blood ; the wafer soaks
It up, and the high priest invokes !

He eats the second Cake.

This Bread I eat. This Oath I swear
As I enflame myself with prayer :

" There is no grace : there is no guilt :
This is the Law : DO WHAT THOU WILT !"

*He strikes Eleven times upon the Bell, and
   cries* ABRAHADABRA.

I entered in with woe ; with mirth
   I now go forth, and with thanksgiving,
To do my pleasure on the earth
   Among the legions of the living.

He goeth forth.

XLV

CHINESE MUSIC

"Explain this happening!"
"It must have a 'natural' cause."
"It must have a 'supernatural' cause." } Let these two asses be set to grind corn.

May, might, must, should, probably, may be, we may safely assume, ought, it is hardly questionable, almost certainly—poor hacks! let them be turned out to grass!

Proof is only possible in mathematics, and mathematics is only a matter of arbitrary conventions.

And yet doubt is a good servant but a bad master; a perfect mistress, but a nagging wife.

"White is white" is the lash of the overseer: "white is black" is the watchword of the slave. The Master takes no heed.

ΚΕΦΑΛΗ ΜF

XLVI

BUTTONS AND ROSETTES

The cause of sorrow is the desire of the One to the Many, or of the Many to the One. This also is the cause of joy.

But the desire of one to another is all of sorrow; its birth is hunger, and its death satiety.

The desire of the moth for the star at least saves him satiety.

Hunger thou, O man, for the infinite : be insatiable even for the finite ; thus at The End shalt thou devour the finite, and become the infinite.

Be thou more greedy that the shark, more full of yearning than the wind among the pines.

The weary pilgrim struggles on ; the satiated pilgrim stops.

The road winds uphill : all law, all nature must be overcome.

Do this by virtue of THAT in thyself before which law and nature are but shadows.

ΚΕΦΑΛΗ ΜΖ

XLVII

WINDMILL-WORDS

Asana gets rid of Anatomy-con-
 sciousness.
Pranayama gets rid of Physiology-
 consciousness.
Yama and Niyama get rid of
 Ethical consciousness.
Pratyhara gets rid of the Objective.
Dharana gets rid of the Subjective.
Dhyana gets rid of the Ego.
Samadhi gets rid of the Soul Impersonal.

Asana destroys the static body (Nama).
Pranayama destroys the dynamic body (Rupa).
Yama destroys the emotions.
Niyama destroys the passions.
Dharana destroys the perceptions
Dhyana destroys the tendencies (Sankhara).
Samadhi destroys the consciousness (Vinnanam
Homard à la Thermidor destroys the digestion.
The last of these facts is the one of which I am
 most certain.

47

ΚΕΦΑΛΗ ΜΗ

XLVIII

MÔME RATHS[22]

The early bird catches the worm and the twelve-year old prostitute attracts the ambassador.
Neglect not the dawn-meditation !

The first plovers' eggs fetch the highest prices; the flower of virginity is esteemed by the pandar.
Neglect not the dawn-meditation !

Early to bed and early to rise
Makes a man healthy and wealthy and wise :
But late to watch and early to pray
Brings him across The Abyss, they say.
Neglect not the dawn-meditation !

ΚΕΦΑΛΗ ΜΘ

XLIX

WARATAH-BLOSSOMS

Seven are the veils of the dancing-girl in the harem of IT.
Seven are the names, and seven are the lamps beside Her bed.
Seven eunuchs guard Her with drawn swords; No Man may come nigh unto Her.
In Her wine-cup are seven streams of the blood of the Seven Spirits of God.
Seven are the heads of THE BEAST whereon She rideth.
The head of an Angel : the head of a Saint : the head of a Poet : the head of An Adulterous Woman : the head of a Man of Valour : the head of a Satyr : and the head of a Lion-Serpent.

Seven letters hath Her holiest name ; and it is

This is the Seal upon the Ring that is on the Forefinger of IT : and it is the Seal upon the Tombs of them whom She hath slain.

Here is Wisdom. Let Him that hath Understanding count the Number of Our Lady ; for it is the Number of a Woman ; and Her Number is

    An Hundred and Fifty and Six.

ΚΕΦΑΛΗ Ν

L

THE VIGIL OF ST. HUBERT

In the forest God met the Stag-beetle. " Hold ! Worship me !" quoth God. " For I am All-Great, All-Good, All Wise . . . . The stars are but sparks from the forges of My smiths . . . ."

" Yea, verily and Amen," said the Stag-beetle, " all this do I believe, and that devoutly."

" Then why do you not worship Me?"

"Because I am real and you are only imaginary."

But the leaves of the forest rustled with the laughter of the wind.

Said Wind and Wood : " They neither of them know anything !"

ΚΕΦΑΛΗ ΝΑ

LI

TERRIER-WORK

Doubt.
Doubt thyself.
Doubt even if thou doubtest thyself.
Doubt all.
Doubt even if thou doubtest all.
It seems sometimes as if beneath all conscious doubt there lay some deepest certainty.
O kill it ! Slay the snake !
The horn of the Doubt-Goat be exalted !
Dive deeper, ever deeper, into the Abyss of Mind, until thou unearth the fox THAT. On, hounds ! Yoicks ! Tally-ho ! Bring THAT to bay !
Then, wind the Mort !

ΚΕΦΑΛΗ ΝΒ

LII

THE BULL-BAITING

Fourscore and eleven books wrote I ; in each did I expound THE GREAT WORK fully, from The beginning even unto The End thereof.

Then at last came certain men unto me, saying: O Master ! Expound thou THE GREAT WORK unto us, O Master !

And I held my peace.

O generation of gossipers ! who shall deliver you from the Wrath that is fallen upon you?

O Babblers, Prattlers, Talkers, Loquacious Ones, Tatlers, Chewers of the Red Rag that inflameth Apis the Redeemer to fury, learn first what is Work ! and THE GREAT WORK is not so far beyond !

ΚΕΦΑΛΗ ΝΓ

LIII

THE DOWSER

Once round the meadow. Brother, does the hazel twig dip?
Twice round the orchard. Brother, does the hazel twig dip?
Thrice round the paddock. Highly, lowly, wily, holy, dip, dip, dip!
Then neighed the horse in the paddock—and lo! its wings.
For whoso findeth the SPRING beneath the earth maketh the treaders-of-earth to course the heavens.
This SPRING is threefold; of water, but also of steel, and of the seasons.
Also this PADDOCK is the Toad that hath the jewel between his eyes—Aum Mani Padmen Hum! (Keep us from Evil!)

ΚΕΦΑΛΗ ΝΔ

LIV

EAVES-DROPPINGS

Five and forty apprentice masons out of work !
Fifteen fellow-craftsmen out of work !
Three Master Masons out of work !
All these sat on their haunches waiting The Report of the Sojourner ; for THE WORD was lost.
This is the Report of the Sojourners : THE WORD was LOVE ;[23] and its number is An Hundred and Eleven.
Then said each AMO ;[24] for its number is An Hundred and Eleven.
Each took the Trowel from his LAP,[25] whose number is An Hundred and Eleven.
Each called moreover on the Goddess NINA,[26] for Her number is An Hundred and Eleven.
Yet with all this went The Work awry ; for THE WORD OF THE LAW IS ΘΕΛΗΜΑ.

ΚΕΦΑΛΗ ΝΕ

LV

THE DROOPING SUNFLOWER

The One Thought vanished ; all my mind was torn to rags : —— nay ! nay ! my head was mashed into wood pulp, and thereon the Daily Newspaper was printed.

Thus wrote I, since my One Love was torn from me. I cannot work : I cannot think : I seek distraction here : I seek distraction there : but this is all my truth, that I *who love have lost ; and how may I regain ?*

I must have money to get to America.

O Mage ! Sage ! Gauge thy Wage, or in the Page of Thine Age is written Rage !

O my darling ! We should not have spent Ninety Pounds in that Three Weeks in Paris ! . . . .

Slash the Breaks on thine arm with a pole-axe !

ΚΕΦΑΛΗ NF

LVI

TROUBLE WITH TWINS

Holy, holy, holy, unto Five Hundred and Fifty Five times holy be OUR LADY of the STARS !

Holy, holy, holy, unto One Hundred and Fifty Six times holy be OUR LADY that rideth upon THE BEAST !

Holy, holy, holy, unto the Number of Times Necessary and Appropriate be OUR LADY Isis in Her Millions-of-Names, All-Mother, Genetrix-Meretrix !

Yet holier than all These to me is LAYLAH, night and death ; for Her do I blaspheme alike the finite and The Infinite.

So wrote not FRATER PERDURABO, but the Imp Crowley in his Name.

For forgery let him suffer Penal Servitude for Seven Years ; or at least let him do Pranayama all the way home—home? nay ! but to the house of the harlot whom he loveth not. For it is LAYLAH that he loveth
. . . .

And yet who knoweth which is Crowley, and which is FRATER PERDURABO?

ΚΕΦΑΛΗ ΝΖ

LVII

THE DUCK-BILLED PLATYPUS

Dirt is matter in the wrong place.
Thought is mind in the wrong place.
Matter is mind ; so thought is dirt.
Thus argued he, the Wise One, not mindful that all place is wrong.
For not until the PLACE is perfected by a T saith he PLACET.
The Rose uncrucified droppeth its petals ; without the Rose the Cross is a dry stick.
Worship then the Rosy Cross, and the Mystery of Two-in-One.
And worship Him that swore by His holy T that One should not be One except in so far as it is Two.
I am glad that LAYLAH is afar ; no doubt clouds love.

ΚΕΦΑΛΗ ΝΗ

LVIII

HAGGAI-HOWLINGS

Haggard am I, an hyaena ; I hunger and howl. Men think it laughter—ha ! ha ! ha !

There is nothing movable or immovable under the firmament of heaven on which I may write the symbols of the secret of my soul.

Yea, though I were lowered by ropes into the utmost Caverns and Vaults of Eternity, there is no word to express even the first whisper of the Initiator in mine ear : yea, I abhor birth, ululating lamentations of Night !

Agony ! Agony ! the Light within me breeds veils ; the song within be dumbness.

God ! in what prism may any man analyse my Light?

Immortal are the adepts ; and yet they die— They die of SHAME unspeakable ; They die as the Gods die, for SORROW.

Wilt thou endure unto The End, O FRATER PERDURABO, O Lamp in The Abyss? Thou hast the Keystone of the Royal Arch ; yet the Apprentices, instead of making bricks, put the straws in their hair, and think they are Jesus Christ !

O sublime tragedy and comedy of THE GREAT WORK !

ΚΕΦΑΛΗ ΝΘ

LIX

THE TAILLESS MONKEY

There is no help—but hotch pot !—in the skies
When Astacus sees Crab and Lobster rise.
Man that has spine, and hopes of heaven-to-be,
Lacks the Amoeba's immortality.
What protoplasm gains in mobile mirth
Is loss of the stability of earth.
Matter and sense and mind have had their day:
Nature presents the bill, and all must pay.
If, as I am not, I were free to choose,
How Buddhahood would battle with The Booze !
My certainty that destiny is " good "
Rests on its picking me for Buddhahood.
Were I a drunkard, I should think I had
Good evidence that fate was " bloody bad."

ΚΕΦΑΛΗ Ξ

LX

THE WOUND OF AMFORTAS[27]

The Self-mastery of Percivale became the Self-masturbatery of the Bourgeois.

Vir-tus has become " virture."

The qualities which have made a man, a race, a city, a caste, must be thrown off : death is the penalty of failure. As it is written : In the hour of success sacrifice that which is dearest to thee unto the Infernal Gods !

The Englishman lives upon the excrement of his forefathers.

All moral codes are worthless in themselves ; yet in every new code there is hope. Provided always that the code is not changed because it is too hard, but because if is fulfilled.

The dead dog floats with the stream ; in puritan France the best women are harlots ; in vicious England the best women are virgins.

If only the Archbishop of Canterbury were to go naked in the streets and beg his bread !

The new Christ, like the old, is the friend of publicans and sinners ; because his nature is ascetic.

O if everyman did No Matter What, provided that it is the one thing that he will not and cannot do !

ΚΕΦΑΛΗ ΞΑ

LXI

THE FOOL'S KNOT

O Fool ! begetter of both I and Naught, resolve this Naught-y Knot !

O ! Ay ! this I and O—IO !—IAO ! For I owe " I " aye to Nibbana's Oe.[28]

I Pay—Pé, the dissolution of the House of God—for Pé comes after O—after Ayin that triumphs over Aleph in Ain, that is O.[29]

OP-us, the Work ! the OP-ening of THE EYE ![30]

Thou Naughty Boy, thou openest THE EYE OF HORUS to the Blind Eye that weeps ![31] The Upright One in thine Uprightness rejoiceth—Death to all Fishes ![32]

ΚΕΦΑΛΗ ΞΒ

LXII

TWIG?[33]

The Phoenix hath a Bell for Sound ; Fire for Sight ; a Knife for Touch ; two cakes, one for taste, the other for smell.

He standeth before the Altar of the Universe at Sunset, when Earth-life fades.

He summons the Universe, and crowns it with MAGICK Light to replace the sun of natural light.

He prays unto, and give homage to, Ro-Hoor-khuit ; to Him he then sacrifices.

The first cake, burnt, illustrates the profit drawn from the scheme of incarnation.

The second, mixt with his life's blood and eaten, illustrates the use of the lower life to feed the higher life.

He then takes the Oath and becomes free—unconditioned—the Absolute.

Burning up in the Flame of his Prayer, and born again—the Phoenix !

LXIII

MARGERY DAW

I love LAYLAH.
I lack LAYLAH.
" Where is the Mystic Grace?" sayest thou?
Who told thee, man, that LAYLAH is not Nuit, and I hadit?
I destroyed all things; they are reborn in other shapes.
I gave up all for One ; this One hath given up its Unity for all?
I wrenched DOG backwards to find GOD ; now GOD barks.
Think me not fallen because I love LAYLAH, and lack LAYLAH.
I am the Master of the Universe ; then give me a heap of straw in a hut, and LAYLAH naked ! Amen.

ΚΕΦΑΛΗ ΞΔ

LXIV

CONSTANCY

I was discussing oysters with a crony :
GOD sent to me the angels DIN and DONI.
" An man of spunk," they urged, " would hardly choose
To breakfast every day chez Lapérouse."
" No !" I replied, " he would not do so, BUT
Think of his woe if Lapérouse were shut !
" I eat these oysters and I drink this wine
Solely to drown this misery of mine.
" Yet the last height of consolation's cold :
Its pinnacle is—not to be consoled !
" And though I sleep with Jane and Eleanor
I feel no better than I did before,
" And Julian only fixes in my mind
Even before feels better than behind.
" You are Mercurial spirits—be so kind
As to enable me to raise the wind.
" Put me in LAYLAH'S arms again : the Accurst,
Leaving me that. elsehow may do his worst."
DONI and DIN, perceiving me inspired,
Conceived their task was finished : they retired.
I turned upon my friend, and, breaking bounds,
Borrowed a trifle of two hundred pounds.

ΚΕΦΑΛΗ ΞΕ

LXV

SIC TRANSEAT ——

" At last I lifted up mine eyes, and beheld ; and lo ! the flames of violet were become as tendrils of smoke, as mist at sunset upon the marsh-lands.

" And in the midst of the moon-pool of silver was the Lily of white and gold. In this Lily is all honey, in this Lily that flowereth at the midnight. In this Lily is all perfume ; in this Lily is all music. And it enfolded me."

Thus the disciples that watched found a dead body kneeling at the altar. Amen !

ΚΕΦΑΛΗ ΞF

LXVI

THE PRAYING MANTIS

" Say : God is One." This I obeyed : for a thousand and one times a night for one thousand nights and one did I affirm the Unity.

But " night " only means LAYLAH ;[34] and Unity and GOD are not worth even her blemishes.

Al-lah is only sixty-six ; but LAYLAH counteth up to Seven and Seventy.[35]

" Yea ! the night shall cover all ; the night shall cover all."

ΚΕΦΑΛΗ ΞZ

LXVII

SODOM-APPLES

I have bought pleasant trifles, and thus soothed my lack of LAYLAH.

Light is my wallet, and my heart is also light ; and yet I know that the clouds will gather closer for the false clearing.

The mirage will fade ; then will the desert be thirstier than before.

O ye who dwell in the Dark Night of the Soul, beware most of all of every herald of the Dawn !

O ye who dwell in the City of the Pyramids beneath the Night of PAN, remember that ye shall see no more light but That of the great fire that shall consume your dust to ashes !

ΚΕΦΑΛΗ ΞΗ

LXVIII

MANNA

At four o'clock there is hardly anybody in Rumpelmayer's.

I have my choice of place and service ; the babble of the apes will begin soon enough.

" Pioneers, O Pioneers !"

Sat not Elijah under the Juniper-tree, and wept?

Was not Mohammed forsaken in Mecca, and Jesus in Gethsemane?

These prophets were sad at heart ; but the chocolate at Rumpelmayer's is great, and the Mousse Noix is like Nepthys for perfection.

Also there are little meringues with cream and chestnut-pulp, very velvety seductions.

Sail I not toward LAYLAH within seven days?

Be not sad at heart, O prophet ; the babble of the apes will presently begin.

Nay, rejoice exceedingly ; for after all the babble of the apes the Silence of the Night.

ΚΕΦΑΛΗ ΞΘ

LXIX

THE WAY TO SUCCEED—AND THE WAY TO SUCK EGGS !

This is the Holy Hexagram.

Plunge from the height, O God, and interlock with Man !

Plunge from the height, O Man, and interlock with Beast !

The Red Triangle is the descending tongue of grace ; the Blue Triangle is the ascending tongue of prayer

This Interchange, the Double Gift of Tongues, the Word of Double Power—ABRAHADABRA!—is the sign of the GREAT WORK, for the GREAT WORK is accomplished in Silence. And behold is not that Word equal to Cheth, that is Cancer. whose Sigil is ♋ ?

This Work also eats up itself, accomplishes its own end, nourishes the worker, leaves no seed, is perfect in itself.

Little children, love one another !

ΚΕΦΑΛΗ Ο

LXX

BROOMSTICK-BABBLINGS

FRATER PERDURABO is of the Sanhedrim of the Sabbath, say men ; He is the Old Goat himself, say women.

Therefore do all adore him ; the more they detest him the more do they adore him.

Ay ! let us offer the Obscene Kiss !

Let us seek the Mystery of the Gnarled Oak, and of the Glacier Torrent !

To Him let us offer up our babes ! Around Him let us dance in the mad moonlight !

But FRATER PERDURABO is nothing but AN EYE ; what eye none knoweth.

Skip, witches ! Hop, toads ! Take your pleasure !—for the play of the Universe is the pleasure of FRATER PERDURABO.

ΚΕΦΑΛΗ ΟΑ

LXXI

KING'S COLLEGE CHAPEL

For mind and body alike there is no purgative like Pranayama, no purgative like Pranayama.

For mind, for body, for mind and body alike—alike !—there is, there is, there is no purgative, no purgative like Pranayama—Pranayama !—Pranayama! yea, for mind and body alike there is no purgative, no purgative, no purgative (for mind and body alike !) no purgative, purgative, purgative like Pranayama, no purgative for mind and body alike, like Pranayama, like Pranayama, like Prana — Prana — Prana — Prana — Pranayama ! Pranayama !

AMEN.

ΚΕΦΑΛΗ ΟΒ

LXXII

HASHED PHEASANT

Shemhamphorash ! all hail, divided Name !
  Utter it once, O mortal over-rash !—
The Universe were swallowed up in flame
  —Shemhamphorash !
Nor deem that thou amid the cosmic crash
  May find one thing of all those things the same !
The world has gone to everlasting smash.

No ! if creation did possess an aim
  (It does not.) it were only to make hash
Of that most " high " and that most holy game,
  Shemhamphorash !

ΚΕΦΑΛΗ ΟΓ

LXXIII

THE DEVIL, THE OSTRICH, AND THE ORPHAN CHILD

Death rides the Camel of Initiation.[36]

Thou humped and stiff-necked one that groanest in Thine Asana, death will relieve thee !

Bite not, Zelator dear, but bide ! Ten days didst thou go with water in thy belly? Thou shalt go twenty more with a firebrand at thy rump !

Ay ! all thine aspiration is to death : death is the crown of all thine aspiration. Triple is the cord of silver moonlight ; it shall hang thee, O Holy One, O Hanged Man, O Camel-Termination-of-the-third-person-plural for thy multiplicity, thou Ghost of a Non-Ego !

Could but Thy mother behold thee, O thou UNT ![37]

The Infinite Snake Ananta that surroundeth the Universe is but the Coffin-Worm !

ΚΕΦΑΛΗ ΟΔ

LXXIV

CAREY STREET

When NOTHING became conscious, it made a bad bargain.
This consciousness acquired individuality : a worse bargain.
The Hermit asked for love ; worst bargain of all.
And now he has let his girl go to America, to have " success " in " life " : blank loss.
Is there no end to this immortal ache
That haunts me, haunts me sleeping or awake?
  If I had Laylah, how could I forget
    Time, Age, and Death? Insufferable fret !
      Were I an hermit, how could I support
      The pain of consciousness, the curse of thought?
        Even were I THAT, there still were one sore spot—
        The Abyss that stretches between THAT and NOT.
Still, the first step is not so far away :—
The Mauretania sails on Saturday !

ΚΕΦΑΛΗ ΟΕ

LXXV

PLOVERS' EGGS[38]

Spring beans and strawberries are in : good-bye to the oyster !
If I really knew what I wanted, I could give up Laylah, or give up everything for Laylah.
But " what I want " varies from hour to hour.
This wavering is the root of all compromise, and so of all good sense.
With this gift a man can spend his seventy years in peace.
Now is this well or ill?
Emphasise *gift*, then *man*, then *spend*, then *seventy years*, and lastly *peace*, and change the intonations—each time reverse the meaning!
I would show you how ; but—for the moment!—I prefer to think of Laylah.

ΚΕΦΑΛΗ O*F*

LXXVI

PHAETON

No.
Yes.
Perhaps.
O !
Eye.
I.
Hi !
Y?
No.
Hail ! all ye spavined, gelded, hamstrung horses !
Ye shall surpass the planets in their courses.
How? Not by speed, nor strength, nor power to stay,
But by the Silence that succeeds the Neigh!

ΚΕΦΑΛΗ OZ

LXXVII

THE SUBLIME AND SUPREME SEPTENARY IN ITS MATURE MAGICAL MANIFESTATION THROUGH MATTER : AS IT IS WRITTEN : AN HE-GOAT ALSO

Laylah.

L.A.Y.L.A.H.

ΚΕΦΑΛΗ ΟΗ

LXXVIII

WHEEL AND—WOA !

The Great Wheel of Samsara.
The Wheel of the Law [Dhamma].
The Wheel of the Taro.
The Wheel of the Heavens.
The Wheel of Life.
All these Wheels be one ; yet of all these the Wheel of the TARO alone avails thee consciously.
Meditate long and broad and deep, O man, upon this Wheel, revolving it in thy mind !
Be this thy task, to see how each card springs necessarily from each other card, even in due order from The Fool unto The Ten of Coins.
Then, when thou know'st the Wheel of Destiny complete, mayst thou perceive THAT Will which moved it first. [There is no first or last.]
And lo ! thou art past through the Abyss.

ΚΕΦΑΛΗ ΟΘ

LXXIX

THE BAL BULLIER

Some men look into their minds into their memories, and find naught but pain and shame.

These then proclaim " The Good Law " unto mankind.

These preach renunciation, " virtue ", cowardice in every form.

These whine eternally.

Smug, toothless, hairless Coote, debauch-emasculated Buddha, come ye to me? I have a trick to make you silent, O ye foamers-at-the mouth !

Nature is wasteful ; but how well She can afford it !

Nature *is* false ; but I'm a bit of a liar myself.

Nature *is* useless ; but then how beautiful she is!

Nature is cruel ; but I too am a Sadist.

The game goes on ; it may have been too rough for Buddha, but it's (if anything) too dull for me.

Viens, beau negre ! Donne-moi tes levres encore!

ΚΕΦΑΛΗ Π

LXXX

BLACKTHORN

The price of existence is eternal warfare.[39]

Speaking as an Irishman, I prefer to say : The price of eternal warfare is existence.

And melancholy as existence is, the price is well worth paying.

Is there is a Government? Then I'm agin it ! To Hell with the bloody English !

" O FRATER PERDURABO, how unworthy are these sentiments ! "

" D'ye want a clip on the jaw? "[40]

LXXXI

LOUIS LINGG

I am not an Anarchist in your sense of the word : your brain is too dense for any known explosive to affect it.

I am not an Anarchist in your sense of the word : fancy a Policeman let loose on Society!

While there exists the burgess, the hunting man, or any man with ideals less than Shelley's and self-discipline less than Loyola's—in short, any man who falls far short of MYSELF—I am against Anarchy, and for Feudalism.

Every " emancipator " has enslaved the free.

LXXXII

BORTSCH

Witch-moon that turnest all the streams to blood,
 I take this hazel rod, and stand, and swear
 An Oath-beneath this blasted Oak and bare
That rears its agony above the flood
  Whose swollen mask mutters an atheist's prayer.
What oath may stand the shock of this offence:
" There is no I, no joy, no permanence "?

Witch-moon of blood, eternal ebb and flow
 Of baffled birth, in death still lurks a change;
 And all the leopards in thy woods that range,
And all the vampires in their boughs that glow,
 Brooding on blood-thirst-these are not so strange
And fierce as life's unfailing shower. These die,
Yet time rebears them through eternity.

Hear then the Oath, witch-moon of blood,
    dread moon !
  Let all thy stryges and thy ghouls attend !
  He that endureth even to the end
Hath sworn that Love's own corpse shall lie
  at noon
  Even in the coffin of its hopes, and spend
All the force won by its old woe and stress
In now annihilating Nothingness.

    This chapter is called Imperial Purple
          and A Punic War.

ΚΕΦΑΛΗ ΠΓ

LXXXIII

THE BLIND PIG[41]

Many becomes two : two one : one Naught.
 What comes to Naught?
What ! shall the Adept give up his hermit life, and go eating and drinking and making merry?
Ay ! shall he not do so? he knows that the Many is Naught ; and having Naught, enjoys that Naught even in the enjoyment of
the Many.
For when Naught becomes Absolute Naught, it becomes again the Many.
Any this Many and this Naught are identical; they are not correlatives or phases of some one deeper Absence-of-Idea ; they are not aspects of some further Light : they are They !
Beware, O my brother, lest this chapter deceive thee !

ΚΕΦΑΛΗ ΠΔ

LXXXIV

THE AVALANCHE

Only through devotion to FRATER PERDURABO may this book be understood.

How much more then should He devote Himself to AIWASS for the understanding of the Holy Books of ΘΕΛΗΜΑ?

Yet must he labour underground eternally. The sun is not for him, nor the flowers, nor the voices of the birds ; for he is past beyond all these. Yea, verily, oft-times he is weary ; it is well that the weight of the Karma of the Infinite is with him.

Therefore is he glad indeed ; for he hath finished THE WORK ; and the reward concerneth him no whit.

ΚΕΦΑΛΗ ΠΕ

LXXXV

BORBORYGMI

I distrust any thoughts uttered by any man whose health is not robust.

All other thoughts are surely symptoms of disease.

Yet these are often beautiful, and may be true within the circle of the conditions of the speaker.

And yet again ! Do we not find that the most robust of men express no thoughts at all? They eat, drink, sleep, and copulate in silence.

What better proof of the fact that all thought is dis-ease?

We are Strassburg geese ; the tastiness of our talk comes from the disorder of our bodies.

We like it ; this only proves that our tastes also are depraved and debauched by our disease.

ΚΕΦΑΛΗ ΠϜ

LXXXVI

TAT

Ex nihilo N. I. H. I. L. fit.

N. the Fire that twisteth itself and burneth like a scorpion.

I. the unsullied ever-flowing water.

H. the interpenetrating Spirit, without and within. Is not its name ABRAHADABRA?

I. the unsullied ever-flowing air.

L. the green fertile earth.

Fierce are the Fires of the Universe, and on their daggers they hold aloft the bleeding heart of earth.

Upon the earth lies water, sensuous and sleepy.

Above the water hangs air ; and above air, but also below fire-and in all-the fabric of all being woven on Its invisible design, is

ΑΙΘΗΡ

ΚΕΦΑΛΗ ΠΖ

LXXXVII

MANDARIN-MEALS

There is a dish of sharks' fins and of sea-slug,
  well set in birds' nests . . . oh !
Also there is a soufflé most exquisite of Chow-
  Chow.
These did I devise.
But I have never tasted anything to match the

which she gave me before She went away.

March 22, 1912.   E. V.

ΚΕΦΑΛΗ ΠΗ

LXXXVIII

GOLD BRICKS

Teach us Your secret, Master ! yap my Yahoos.

Then for the hardness of their hearts, and for the softness of their heads, I taught them Magick.

But . . . . alas !

Teach us Your real secret, Master ! how to become invisible, how to acquire love, and oh ! beyond all, how to make gold.

But how much gold will you give me for the Secret of Infinite Riches?

Then said the foremost and most foolish ; Master, it is nothing ; but here is an hundred thousand pounds.

This did I deign to accept, and whispered in his ear this secret :

A SUCKER IS BORN EVERY MINUTE.

ΚΕΦΑΛΗ ΠΘ

LXXXIX

UNPROFESSIONAL CONDUCT

I am annoyed about the number 89.
I shall avenge myself by writing nothing in this chapter.
That, too, is wise ; for since I am annoyed, I could not write even a reasonably decent lie.

ΚΕΦΑΛΗ Ρ

XC

STARLIGHT

Behold! I have lived many years, and I have travelled in every land that is under the dominion of the Sun, and I have sailed the seas from pole to pole.

Now do I lift up my voice and testify that all is vanity on earth, except the love of a good woman, and that good woman LAYLAH. And I testify that in heaven all is vanity (for I have journeyed oft, and sojourned oft, in every heaven), except the love of OUR LADY BABALON. And I testify that beyond heaven and earth is the love of OUR LADY NUIT.

And seeing that I am old and well stricken in years, and that my natural forces fail, therefore do I rise up in my throne and call upon THE END.

For I am youth eternal and force infinite.

And at THE END is SHE that was LAY-LAH, and BABALON, and NUIT, being . . . .

ΚΕΦΑΛΗ ΡΑ

XCI

THE HEIKLE

A. M. E. N.

NOTES

1. Silence. Nuit, O ; Hadit ; Ra-Hoor-Khuit, I.
2. The Unbroken, absorbing all, is called Darkness.
3. Fourteen letters. Quid Voles Illud Fac. Q.V.I.F. $196=14_2$.
4. They cause all men to worship it.
5. Masters of the Temple, whose grade has the mystic number 6 (=1+2+3).
6. These are not eight, as apparent ; for Lao-tze counts as 0.
7. The legend of " Christ " is only a corruption and perversion of other legends. Especially of Dionysus : compare the account of Christ before Herod/Pilate in the Gospels, and of Dionysus before Pentheus in the Bacchae.
8. O, the last letter of Perdurabo, is Naught.
9. $2001=11\ \Sigma(1-13)$. The Petals of the Sahasrara-cakkra.
10. JOY=101, the Egg of Spirit in equilibrium between the Pillars of the Temple.
11. This chapter must be read in connection with Wagner's " Parsifal."
12. O=Vζ, " The Devil of the Sabbath." U=8, the Hierophant or Redeemer. T=Strength, the Lion.
13. T, manhood, the sign of the cross or phallus. UT, the Holy Guardian Angel ; UT, the first syllable of Udgita, see the Upanishads. O, Nothing or Nuit.

14. The secret sense of these words is to be sought in the numberation thereof.
15. In nature the Tortoise has 6 members at angles of 60°.
16. I.e. the truth that he hath slept.
17. His initials I. B. M. are the initials of the Three Pillars of the Temple, and add to 52, 13X4, BN, the Son.
18. This chapter was written to clarify χεφ-ιδ, of which it was the origin. FRATER PERDURABO perceived this truth, or rather the first half of it, comedy, at breakfast at " Au Chien qui Fume."
19. HIMOG is a Notariqon of the words Holy Illuminated Man of God.
20. *I.e.* food suitable for Americans.
21. Turbulence is here specially used to suggest " tourbillon."
22. " The môme raths outgrabe."—Lewis Carroll. But " môme " is Parisian slang for a young girl, and " rathe " O. E. for early. " The rathe primrose."—Milton.
23. L=30, O=70, V=6, E=5=111.
24. A=1, M=40, O=70=111.
25. The trowel is shaped like a diamond or Yoni. L=30, A=1, P=80=111
26 N=50, I=10, N=50, A=1=111.
27. Chapter so called because Amfortas was wounded by his own spear, the spear that had made him king.

28. Oe=Island, a common symbol of Nibbana.
29. אין Ain. עין Ayin.
30. Scil. of Shiva.
31. Cf. Bagh-i-Muattar for all this symbolism.
32. Death=Nun, the letter before O, means a fish, a symbol of Christ, and also by its shape the Female principle.
33. Twig? =dost thou understand? Also the Phoenix takes twigs to kindle the fire in which it burns itself.
34. Laylah is the Arabic for night.
35.   =1+30+30+5=66   L+A+I+L+A+H=77, which also gives MZL, the Influence of the Highest, OZ, a goat, and so on.
36. Death is said by the Arabs to ride a Camel. The Path of Gimel (which means a Camel) leads from Tiphareth to Kether, and its Tarot trump is the "High Priestess."
37. UNT, Hindustani for Camel. I.e. Would that BABALON might look on thee with favour.
38. These eggs being speckled, resemble the wandering mind referred to.
39. ISVD, the foundation scil. of the universe=80=P, the letter of Mars.
40. P also means "a mouth."
41. πγ=PG=Pig without an I=Blind Pig.

PRO AND CON TENTS

0 0
  0

1. The Sabbath of the Goat
2. The Cry of the Hawk.
3. The Oyster.
4. Peaches.
5. The Battle of the Ants.
6. Caviar.
7. The Dinosaurs.
8. Steeped Horsehair.
9. The Branks.
10. Windlestraws
11. The Glow-Worm.
12. The Dragon-Flies.
13. Pilgrim-Talk.
14. Onion-Peelings.
15. The Gun-Barrel.
16. The Stag-Beetle.
17. The Swan.
18. Dewdrops.
19. The Leopard and the Deer.
20. Samson.
21. The Blind Webster.
22. The Despot.
23. Skidoo !
24. The Hawk and the Blindworm
25. THE STAR RUBY.
26. The Elephant and the Tortoise.
27. The Sorcerer.
28. The Pole-Star
29. The Southern Cross.
30. John-a-Dreams.
31. The Garotte.
32. The Mountaineer.
33. BAPHOMET.
34. The Smoking Dog.
35. Venus of Milo.
36. THE STAR SAPPHIRE.
37. Dragons.
38. Lambskin.
39. The Looby.
40. The HIMOG.
41. Corn Beef Hash.
42. Dust-Devils.
43. Mulberry Tops.
44. THE MASS OF THE PHOENIX.

45. Chinese Music.
46. Buttons and Rosettes.
47. Windmill-Words.
48. Môme Raths.
49. WARATAH-BLOSSOMS.
50. The Vigil of St. Hubert.
51. Terrier Work.
52. The Bull-Baiting.
53. The Dowser.
54. Eaves-Droppings.
55. The Drooping Sunflower.
56. Trouble with Twins.
57. The Duck - Billed Platypus
58. Haggai-Howlings.
59. The Tailless Monkey.
60. The Wound of Amfortas.
61. The Fool's Knot.
62. Twig?
63. Margery Daw.
64. Constancy.
65. Sic Transeat——
66. The Praying Mantis.
67. Sodom-Apples.
68. Manna.
69. The Way to Succeed —and the Way to Suck Eggs !
70. Broomstick-Babblings.
71. King's College Chapel.
72. Hashed Pheasant.
73. The Devil, The Ostrich, and the Orphan Child.
74. Carey Street.
75. Plover's Eggs.
76. Phaeton.
77. THE SUBLIME AND SUPREME SEPTENARY IN ITS MATURE MAGICAL MANIFESTATION THROUGH MATTER : AS IT IS WRITTEN : AN HE-GOAT ALSO.
78. Wheel and—Woa !
79. The Bal Bullier.
80. Blackthorn.
81. Louis Lingg.
82. Bortsch : also Imperial Purple (and A PUNIC WAR).
83. The Blind Pig.
84. The Avalanche.
85. Borborygmi.
86. TAT.
87. Mandarin-Meals.
88. Gold Bricks.
89. Unprofessional Conduct.
90. Starlight.
91. The Heikle.

Commentaries on 'The Book of Lies'.

Aleister Crowley

1923

Commentaries.

0

The Chapter that is not a Chapter

THIS CHAPTER, numbered 0, corresponds to the Negative, which is before Kether in the Qabalistic system. The notes of interrogation and exclamation on the previous pages are the other two veils. The meaning of these symbols is fully explained in "The Soldier and the Hunchback". This chapter begins by the letter O, followed by a mark of exclamation; its reference to the theogony of "Liber Legis" is explained in the note, but it also refers to *KTEIS PHALLOS* and *SPERMA*, and is the exclamation of wonder or ecstasy, which is the ultimate nature of things.

Commentaries.

The Ante Primal Triad

THIS IS THE NEGATIVE TRINITY; its three statements are, in an ultimate sense, identical. They harmonise Being, Becoming, Not-Being, the three possible modes of conceiving the universe. The statement, Nothing is Not, technically equivalent to Something Is, is fully explained in the essay called Berashith. The rest of the chapter follows the Sephirotic system of the Qabalah, and constitutes a sort of quintessential comment upon that system. Those familiar with that system will recognise Kether, Chokmah, Binah, in the First Triad; Daath, in the Abyss; Chesed, Geburah, Tiphareth, in the Second Triad; Netzach, Hod and Yesod in the Third Triad, and Malkuth in the Tenth Emanation. It will be noticed that this cosmogony is very complete; the manifestation even of God does not appear until Tiphareth; and the universe itself not until Malkuth. The chapter many therefore be considered as the most complete treatise on existence ever written.

Commentaries.

I

Sabbath of the Goat

THE SHAPE OF THE FIGURE 'I' suggests the Phallus; this chapter is therefore called the Sabbath of the Goat, the Witches' Sabbath, in which the Phallus is adored. The chapter begins with a repetition of O! referred to in the previous chapter. It is explained that this triad lives in Night, the Night of Pan, which is mystically called N.O.X., and this O is identified with the O in this word. N is the Tarot symbol, Death; and the X or Cross is the sign of the Phallus. For a fuller commentary on Nox, see Liber VII, Chapter I. Nox adds to 210, which symbolises the reduction of duality to unity, and thence to negativity, and is thus a hieroglyph of the Great Work. The word Pan is then explained, Π, the letter of Mars, is a hieroglyph of two pillars, and therefore suggest duality; A, by its shape, is the pentagram, energy, and N, by its Tarot attribution, is death. Nox is then further explained, and it is shown that the ultimate Trinity, O!, is supported, or fed, by the process of death and begetting, which are the laws of the universe. The identity of these two is then explained. The Student is then charged to understand the spiritual importance of this physical procession in line 5. It

Commentaries.

is then asserted that the ultimate letter A has two names, or phases, Life and Death. Line 7 balances line 5. It will be notice that the phraseology of these two lines is so conceived that the one contains the other more than itself. Line 8 emphasises the importance of performing both.

Commentaries.

II

The Cry of the Hawk

THE "HAWK" REFERRED TO IS HORUS. The chapter begins with a comment on Liber Legis III, 49. Those four words, Do What Thou Wilt, are also identified with the four possible modes of conceiving the universe; Horus unites these. Follows a version of the "Lord's Prayer", suitable to Horus. Compare this with the version in Chapter 44. There are ten sections in this prayer, and, as the prayer is attributed to Horus, they are called four, as above explained; but it is only the name of Horus which is fourfold; He himself is One. This may be compared with the Qabalistic doctrine of the Ten Sephiroth as an expression of Tetragrammaton (1 plus 2 plus 3 plus 4 = 10). It is now seen that this Hawk is not Solar, but Mercurial; hence the words, the Cry of the Hawk, the essential part of Mercury being his Voice; and the number of the chapter, B, which is Beth the letter of Mercury, the Magus of the Tarot, who has four weapons, and it must be remembered that this card is numbered 1, again connecting all these symbols with the Phallus. The essential weapon of Mercury is the Caduceus.

Commentaries.

III

The Oyster

GIMEL IS THE HIGH PRIESTESS of the Tarot. This chapter gives the initiated feminine point of view; it is therefore called the Oyster, a symbol of the Yoni. In Equinox X, The Temple of Solomon the King, it is explained how Masters of the Temple, or Brothers of A∴ A∴. have changed the formula of their progress. These two formulae, Solve et Coagula, are now explained, and the universe is exhibited as the interplay between these two. This also explains the statement in Liber Legis I, 28-30.

Commentaries.

IV

Peaches

Daleth is the Empress of the Tarot, the letter of Venus, and the title, Peaches, again refers to the Yoni. The chapter is a counsel to accept all impressions; it is the formula of the Scarlet woman; but no impression must be allowed to dominate you, only to fructify you; just as the artist, seeing an object, does not worship it, but breeds a masterpiece from it. This process is exhibited as one aspect of the Great Work. The last two paragraphs may have some reference to the 13th Aethyr (see The Vision and The Voice).

Commentaries.

V

The Battle of the Ants

HE IS THE LETTER OF ARIES, a Martial sign; while the title suggests war. The ants are chosen as small busy objects. Yet He, being a holy letter, raises the beginning of the chapter to a contemplation of the Pentagram, considered as a glyph of the ultimate. In line 1, Being is identified with Not-Being. In line 2, Speech with Silence. In line 3, the Logos is declared as the Negative. Line 4 is another phrasing of the familiar Hindu statement, that that which can be thought is not true. In line 5, we come to an important statement, an adumbration of the most daring thesis in this book- Father and Son are not really two, but one; their unity being the Holy Ghost, the semen; the human form is a non-essential accretion of this quintessence. So far the chapter has followed the Sephiroth from Kether to Chesed, and Chesed is united to the Supernal Triad by virtue of its Phallic nature; for not only is Amoun a Phallic God, and Jupiter the Father of All, but 4 is Daleth, Venus, and Chesed refers to water, from which Venus sprang, and which is the symbol of the Mother in the Tetragrammaton. See Chapter 0, "God the Father and Mother is concealed in generation". But Chesed, in the lower sense, is conjoined to Microprosopus. It is the true link

Commentaries.

between the greater and lesser countenances, whereas Daath is the false. Compare the doctrine of the higher and lower Manas in Theosophy. The rest of the chapter therefor points out the duality, and therefore the imperfection, of all the lower Sephiroth in their essence.

Commentaries.

VI

Caviar

THIS CHAPTER IS PRESUMABLY called Caviar because that substance is composed of many spheres. The account given of Creation is the same as that familiar to students of the Christian tradition, the Logos transforming the unity into the many. We then see what different classes of people do with the many. The Rationalist takes the six Sephiroth of Microprosopus in a crude state, and declares them to be the universe. This folly is due to the pride of reason. The Adept concentrates the Microcosm in Tiphareth, recognising an Unity, even in the microcosm, but, qua Adept, he can go no further. The Master of the Temple destroys all these illusions, but remains silent. See the description of his functions in the Equinox, Liber 418 and elsewhere. In the next grade, the Word is reformulated, for the Magus in Chokmah, the Dyad, the Logos. The Ipsissimus, in the highest grade of the A∴ A∴ is totally unconscious of this process, or, it might be better to say, he 108ecognizes it as Nothing, in that positive sense of the word, which is only intelligible in Samasamadhi.

Commentaries.

VIII

Steeped Horsehair

THIS CHAPTER GIVES A LIST OF those special messengers of the Infinite who initiate periods. they are called Dinosaurs because of their seeming to be terrible devouring creatures. They are Masters of the Temple, for their number is 6 (1 plus 2 plus 3), the mystic number of Binah; but they are called "None", because they have attained. If it were not so, they would be called "six" in its bad sense of mere intellect. They are called Seven, although they are Eight, because Lao-tzu counts as nought, owing to the nature of his doctrine. The reference to their "living not" is to be found in Liber 418. The word "Perdurabo" means "I will endure unto the end". The allusion is explained in the note. Siddartha, or Gotama, was the name of the last Budda. Krishna was the principal incarnation of the Indian Vishnu, the preserver, the principal expounder of Vedantism. Tahuti, or Thoth, the Egyptian God of Wisdom. Mosheh, Moses, the founder of the Hebrew system. Dionysus, probably an ecstatic from the East. Mahmud, Mohammed. All these were men; their Godhead is the result of mythopoeia.

Cheth is the Chariot in the Tarot. The Charioteer is the bearer of the Holy Grail. All

Commentaries.

this should be studied in Liber 418, the 12th Aethyr. The chapter is called "Steeped Horsehair" because of the mediaeval tradition that by steeping horsehair a snake is produced, and the snake is the hieroplyphic representation of semen, particularly in Gnostic and Egyptian emblems. The meaning of the chapter is quite clear; the whole consciousness, that which is omnipotent, omniscient, omnipresent, is hidden therein. Therefore, except in the case of an Adept, man only rises to a glimmer of the universal consciousness, while, in the orgasm, the mind is blotted out.

Commentaries.

IX

The Branks

TETH IS THE TAROT TRUMP, Strength, in which a woman is represented closing the mouth of a lion. This chapter is called "The Branks", an even more powerful symbol, for it is the Scottish, and only known, apparatus for closing the mouth. The chapter is formally an attack upon the parts of speech, the interjection, the meaningless utterance of ecstasy, being the only thing worth saying; yet even this is to be regarded as a lapse. "Aum" represents the entering into the silence, as will observed upon pronouncing it.

Commentaries.

X

Windlestraws

THERE IS NO APPARENT connection between the number of this chapter and its subject. It does, however, refer to the key of the Tarot called The Hermit, which represents him as cloaked. Jod is the concealed Phallus as opposed to Tau, the extended Phallus. This chapter should be studied in the light of what is said in "Aha!" and in the Temple of Solomon the King about the reason. The universe is insane, the law of cause and effect is an illusion, or so it appears in the Abyss, which is thus identified with consciousness, the many, and both; but within this is a secret unity which rejoices; this unit being far beyond any conception.

Commentaries.

XI

The Glow-worm

"The Glow-Worm" may perhaps be translated as "a little light in the darkness", though there may be a subtle reference to the nature of that light. Eleven is the great number of Magick, and this chapter indicates a supreme magical method; but it is really called eleven, because of Liber Legis, I, 60. The first part of the chapter describes the universe in its highest sense, down to Tiphareth; it is the new and perfect cosmogony of Liber Legis. Chaos and Babalon are Chokmah and Binah, but they are really one; the essential unity of the supernal Triad is here insisted upon. Pan is a generic name, including this whole system of its manifested side. Those which are above the Abyss are therefore said to live in the Night of Pan; they are only reached by the annihilation of the All. Thus, the Master of the Temple lives in the Night of Pan. Now, below the Abyss, the manifested part of the Master of the temple, also reaches Samadhi, as the way of Annihilation. Paragraph 7 begins by a reflection produced by the preceding exposition. This reflection is immediately contradicted, the author being a Master of the Temple. He thereupon enters into his Samadhi, and he piles contradiction upon contradiction,

Commentaries.

and thus a higher degree of rapture, with ever sentence, until his armoury is exhausted, and, with the word Amen, he enters the supreme state.

Commentaries.

XII

The Dragon-Flies

THE DRAGON-FLIES WERE CHOSEN as symbols of joy, because of the author's observation as a naturalist. Paragraph 1 mere repeats Chapter 4 in quintessence; 1001, being 11 Σ (1-13), is a symbol of the complete unity manifested as the many, for Σ (1-13) gives the whole course of numbers from the simple unity of 1 to the complex unity of 13, impregnated by the magical 11. I may add a further comment on the number 91. 13 (1 plus 3) is a higher form of 4. 4 is Amoun, the God of generation, and 13 is 1, the Phallic unity. Daleth is the Yoni. And 91 is AMN (Amen), a form of the Phallus made complete through the intervention of the Yoni. This again connects with the IO and OI of paragraph 1, and of course IO is the rapture-cry of the Greeks. The whole chapter is, again, a comment on Liber legis, 1, 28-30.

Commentaries.

XIII

Pilgrim-talk

THIS CHAPTER IS PERFECTLY CLEAR to anyone who has studied the career of an Adept. The Sodom-Apple is an uneatable fruit found in the desert.

Commentaries.

XIV

Onion-peelings

THE TITLE, "ONION-PEELINGS", refers to the well-known incident in "Peer Gynt". The chapter resembles strongly Dupin's account of how he was able to win at the game of guessing odd or even. (See Poe's tale of "The Purloined Letter".) But this is a more serious piece of psychology. In one's advance towards a comprehension of the universe, one changes radically one's point of view; nearly always it amounts to a reversal. This is the cause of most religious controversies. Paragraph 1, however, is Frater Perdurabo's formula- tion of his perception of the Universal Joke, also described in Chapter 34. All individual existence is tragic. Perception of this fact is the essence of comedy. "Household Gods" is an attempt to write pure comedy. "The Bacchae" of Euripides is another. At the end of the chapter it is, however, seen that to the Master of the Temple the opposite perception occurs simultaneously, and that he himself is beyond both of these. And in the last paragraph it is shown that he 117ealizes the truth as beyond any statement of it.

Commentaries.

XV

The Gun Barrell

THE CARD 15 IN THE TAROT is "The Devil", the mediaeval blind for Pan. The title of the chapter refers to the Phallus, which is here identified with the will. The Greek word Πυραμις has the same number as Φαλλος. This chapter is quite clear, but one my remark in the last paragraph a reference to the nature of Samadhi. As man loses his personality in physical love, so does the magician annihilate his divine personality in that which is beyond. The formula of Samadhi is the same, from the lowest to the highest. The Rosy-Cross is the Universal Key. But, as one proceeds, the Cross becomes greater, until it is the Ace, the Rose, until it is the Word.

Commentaries.

XVIII

Dewdrops

THE 18TH KEY OF THE TAROT refers to the Moon, which was supposed to shed dew. The appropriateness of the chapter title is obvious. The chapter must be read in connection with Chapters 1 and 16. I the penultimate paragraph, Vindu is identified with Amrita, and in the last paragraph the disciple is charged to let it have its own way. It has a will of its own, which is more in accordance with the Cosmic Will, than that of the man who is its guardian and servant.

Commentaries.

XIX

The Leopard and the Deer

19 IS THE LAST TRUMP, "The Sun', which is the representative of god in the Macrocosm, as the Phallus is in the Microcosm. There is a certain universality and adaptability among its secret power. The chapter is taken from Rudyard Kiplin's "Just So Stories". The Master urges his disciples to a certain holy stealth, a concealment of the real purpose of their lives; in this way making the best of both worlds. This counsels a course of action hardly distinguishable from hypocrisy; but the distinction is obvious to any clear thinker, though not altogether so the Frater P.

Commentaries.

XX

Sampson

SAMSON, THE HEBREW HERCULES, is said in the legend to have pulled down the walls of a music-hall where he was engaged, "to make sport for the Philistines", destroying them and himself. Milton founds a poem on this fable. The first paragraph is a corollary of Newton's First Law of Motion. The key to infinite power is to reach the Bornless Beyond.

Commentaries.

XXI

The Blind Webster

THE 21ST KEY OF THE TAROT is called "The Universe", and refers to the letter Tau, the Phallus in manifestation; hence the title, "The Blind Webster". The universe is conceived as Buddhists, on the one hand, and Rationalists, on the other, would have us do; fatal, and without intelligence. Even so, it may be delightful to the creator. The moral of this chapter is, therefore, and exposition of the last paragraph of Chapter 18. It is the critical spirit which is the Devil, and gives rise to the appearance of evil.

Commentaries.

XXII

The Despot

COMMENT WOULD ONLY MAR the supreme simplicity of this chapter.

Commentaries.

XXIII

Skidoo

BOTH "23" AND "SKIDOO" are American words meaning "Get out". This chapter describes the Great Work under the figure of a man ridding himself of all his accidents. He first leaves the life of comfort; then the world at large; and, lastly, even the initiates. In the fourth section is shown that there is no return for one that has started on this path. The word OUT is then analysed, and treated as a noun. Besides the explanation in the note, O is the Yoni; T, the Lingam; and U, the Hierophant; the 5th card of the Tarot, the Pentagram. It is thus practically identical with IAO. The rest of the chapter is clear, for the note.

Commentaries.

XXIV

The Hawk and the Blind-worm

THE HAWK IS THE SYMBOL OF SIGHT; the Blindworm, of blindness. Those who are under the dominion of reason are called blind. In the last paragraph is reasserted the doctrine of Chapters 1, 8, 16 and 18. For the meaning of the word hriliu consult Liber 418.

Commentaries.

XXV

The Star Ruby

25 IS THE SQUARE OF 5, and the Pentagram has the red colour of Geburah. The chapter is a new and more elaborate version of the Banishing Ritual of the Pentagram. It would be improper to comment further upon an official ritual of the A∴ A∴.

Commentaries.

XXVI

The Elephant and the Tortoise

THE TITLE OF THE CHAPTER refers to the Hindu legend. The first paragraph should be read in connection with our previous remarks upon the number 91. The number of the chapter, 26, is that of Tetragrammaton, the manifest creator, Jehovah. He is called the Second in relation to that which is above the Abyss, comprehended under the title of the First. But the vulgarians conceive of nothing beyond the creator, and therefore call him The First. He is really the Fourth, being in Chesed, and of course his nature is fourfold. This Four is conceived of as the Dyad multiplied by the Dyad; falsehood con- firming falsehood. Paragraph 3 introduces a new conception; that of the square within the hexagram, the universe enclosed in the law of Lingam-Yoni. The penultimate paragraph shows the redemption of the universe by this law. The figure 10, like the work IO, again suggest Lingam-Yoni, besides the exclamation given in the text. The last paragraph curses the universe thus unredeemed. The eleven initial A's in the last sentence are Magick Pentagrams, emphasising this curse.

Commentaries.

XXVII

The Sorcerer

THIS CHAPTER GIVES the reverse of the medal; it is the contrast to Chapter 15. The Sorcerer is to be identified with The Brother of the Left Hand Path.

Commentaries.

XXVIII

The Pole-star

This now introduces the principal character of this book, **Laylah**, who is the ultimate feminine symbol, to be interpreted on all planes. But in this chapter, little hint is given of anything beyond physical love. It is called the Pole-Star, because **Laylah** is the one object of devotion to which the author ever turns. Note the introduction of the name of the Beloved in acrostic in line 15.

Commentaries.

XXIX

The Southern Cross

CHAPTER 29 CONTINUES CHAPTER 28. Note that the word **Laylah** is the Arabic for "Night". The author begins to identify the Beloved with the N.O.X. previously spoken of. the chapter is called "The Southern Cross", because, on the physical plane, **Laylah** is an Australian.

Commentaries.

XXX

John-a-dreams

THIS CHAPTER IS TO BE READ in connection with Chapter 8, and also with those previous chapters in which the reason is attacked. The allusion in the title is obvious. This sum in proportion, dream: waking: : waking: Samadhi is a favourite analogy with Frater P., who frequently employs it in his holy discourse.

Commentaries.

XXXI

The Garotte

THE NUMBER 31 REFERS to the Hebrew word LA, which means "not". A new character is now introduce under the title of IT, I being the secret, and T being the manifested, phallus. This is, however, only one aspect of IT, which may perhaps be defined as the Ultimate Reality. IT is apparently a more exalted thing than THAT. This chapter should be compared with Chapter 11; that method of destroying the reason by formulating contradictions is definitely inculcated. The reason is situated in Daath, which corresponds the the throat in human anatomy. Hence the title of the chapter, "The Garotte". The idea is that, by forcing the mind to follow, and as far as possible to realise, the language of Beyond the Abyss, the student will succeed in bringing his reason under control. As soon as the reason is vanquished, the garotte is removed; then the influence of the supernals (Kether, Chokmah, Binah), no longer inhibited by Daath, can descend upon Tiphareth, where the human will is situated, and flood it with the ineffable light.

Commentaries.

XXXII

The Mountaineer

THIS TITLE IS A MERE REFERENCE to the metaphor of the last paragraph of the chapter. Frater P., as is well known, is a mountaineer. This chapter should be read in conjunction with Chapters 8 and 30. It is a practical instruction, the gist of which is easily to be apprehended by comparatively short practice of Mantra-Yoga. A mantra is not being properly said as long as the man knows he is saying it. The same applies to all other forms of Magick.

Commentaries.

XXXIII

Baphomet

33 IS THE NUMBER OF THE Last Degree of Masonry, which was conferred upon Frater P. in the year 1900 of the vulgar era by Don Jesus de Medina-Sidonia in the City of Mexico. Baphomet is the mysterious name of the God of the Templars. The Eagle described in paragraph 1 is that of the Templars. This Masonic symbol is, however, identified by Frater P. with a bird, which is master of the four elements, and therefore of the name Tetragrammaton. Jacobus Burgundus Molensis suffered martyrdom in the City of Paris in the year 1314 of the vulgar era. The secrets of his order were, however, not lost, and are still being communicated to the worthy by his successors, as is intimated by the last paragraph, which implies knowledge of a secret worship, of which the Grand Master did not speak. The Eagle may be identified, though not too closely, with the Hawk previously spoken of. It is perhaps the Sun, the exoteric object of worship of all sensible cults; it is not to be confused with other objects of the mystic aviary, such as the swan, phoenix, pelican, dove and so on.

Commentaries.

XXXIV

The Smoking Dog

THE TITLE IS EXPLAINED IN THE NOTE. The chapter needs no explanation; it is a definite point of view of life, and recommends a course of action calculated to rob the creator of his cruel sport.

Commentaries.

XXXV

Venus of Milo

THIS CHAPTER MUST BE READ in connection with Chapters 1, 3, 4, 8, 15, 16, 18, 24, 28, 29. The last sentence of paragraph 4 also connects with the first paragraph of Chapter 26. The title "Venus of Milo" is an argument in support of paragraphs 1 and 2, it being evident from this statement that the male body becomes beautiful in so far as it approximates to the female. The female is to be regarded as having been separated from the male, in order to reproduce the male in a superior form, the absolute, and the conditions forming the one absolute. In the last two paragraphs there is a justification of a practice which might be called sacred prostitution. In the common practice of meditation the idea is to reject all impressions, but here is an opposite practice, very much more difficult, in which all are accepted. This cannot be done at all unless one is capable of making Dhyana at least on any conceivable thing, at a second's notice; otherwise, the practice would only be ordinary mind-wandering.

Commentaries.

XXXVI

The Star Sapphire

THE STAR SAPPHIRE corresponds with the Star-Ruby of Chapter 25; 36 being the square of 6, as 25 is of 5. This chapter gives the real and perfect Ritual of the Hexagram. It would be improper to comment further upon an official ritual of the A∴ A∴.

Commentaries.

XXXVII

Dragons

DRAGONS ARE IN THE EAST supposed to cause eclipses by devouring the luminaries. There may be some significance in the chapter number, which is that of Jechidah the highest unity of the soul. In this chapter, the idea is given that all limitation and evil is an exceedingly rare accident; there can be no night in the whole of the Solar System, except in rare spots, where the shadow of a planet is cast by itself. It is a serious misfortune that we happen to live in a tiny corner of the system, where the darkness reaches such a high figure as 50 percent. The same is true of moral and spiritual conditions.

Commentaries.

XXXVIII

Lambskin

THIS CHAPTER WILL BE readily intelligible to E.A. Freemasons, and it cannot be explained to others.

Commentaries.

XXXIX

The Looby

THE WORD LOOBY occurs in folklore, and was supposed to be the author, at the time of writing this book, which he did when he was far from any standard works of reference, to connote partly "booby", partly "lout". It would thus be a similar word to "Parsifal". Paragraphs 2-6 explain the method that was given in Chapters 11 and 31. This method, however, occurs throughout the book on numerous occasions, and even in the chapter itself it is employed in the last paragraphs.

Commentaries.

XL

The HIMOG

PARAGRAPH 1 IS, OF COURSE, a well-known scientific fact. In paragraph 2 it is suggested analogically that all thinkable things are similarly blinds for the Unthinkable Reality. Classing in this manner all things as illusions, the question arises as to the distinguishing between illusions; how are we to tell whether a Holy Illuminated Man of God is really so, since we can see nothing of him but his imperfections. It may be yonder beggar is a King." But these considerations are not to trouble such mind as the Chela may possess; let him occupy himself, rather, with the task of getting rid of his personality; this, and not criticism of his holy Guru, should be the occupation of his days and nights.

Commentaries.

XLI

Corn Beef Hash

THE TITLE IS ONLY partially explained in the note; it means that the statements in this chapter are to be understood in the most ordinary and commonplace way, without any mystical sense. V.V.V.V.V. is the motto of a Master of the Temple (or so much He disclosed to the Exempt Adepts), referred to in Liber LXI. It is he who is responsible for the whole of the development of the A∴ A∴ movement which has been associated with the publication of *THE EQUINOX*; and His utterance is enshrined in the sacred writings. It is useless to enquire into His nature; to do so leads to certain disaster. Authority from him is exhibited, when necessary, to the proper persons, though in no case to anyone below the grade of Exempt Adept. The person enquiring into such matters is politely requested to work, and not to ask questions about matters which in no way concern him. The number 41 is that of the Barren Mother.

Commentaries.

XLII

Dust-devils

THIS NUMBER 42 is the Great Number of the Curse. See Liber 418, Liber 500, and the essay on the Qabalah in the Temple of Solomon the King. This number is said to be all hotch-potch and accursed. The chapter should be read most carefully in connection with the 10th Aethyr. It is to that dramatic experience that it refers. The mind is called "wind", because of its nature; as has been frequently explained, the ideas and words are identical. In this free-flowing, centreless material arises an eddy; a spiral close-coiled upon itself. The theory of the formation of the Ego is that of the Hindus, whose Ahamkara is itself a function of the mind, whose ego it creates. This Ego is entirely divine. Zoroaster describes God as having the head of the Hawk, and a spiral force. It will be difficult to understand this chapter with- out some experience in the transvaluation of values, which occurs throughout the whole of this book, in nearly every other sentence. Transvaluation of values is only the moral aspect of the method of contradiction. The word "turbulence" is applied to the Ego to suggest the French "tourbillion", whirlwind, the false Ego or dust-devil. True life, the life, which has no consciousness of "I", is said to

Commentaries.

be choked by this false ego, or rather by the thoughts which its explosions produce. In paragraph 4 this is expanded to a macrocosmic plane. The Masters of the Temple are now introduced; they are inhabitants, not of this desert; their abode is not this universe. They come from the Great Sea, Binah, the City of the Pyramids. V.V.V.V.V. is indicated as one of these travellers; He is described as a camel, not because of the connotation of the French form of this word, but because "camel" is in Hebrew Gimel, and Gimel is the path leading from Tiphareth to Kether, uniting Microprosopus and Macroprosopus, i.e. performing the Great Work. The card Gimel in the Tarot is the High Priestess, the Lady of Initiation; one might even say, the Holy Guardian Angel.

Commentaries.

XLIII

Mulberry Tops

THE TITLE OF THIS CHAPTER refers to a Hebrew legend, that of the prophet who heard "a going in the mulberry tops"; and to Browning's phrase, "a bruised, black-blooded mulberry". In the World's Tragedy, Household Gods, The Scorpion, and also The God-Eater, the reader may study the efficacy of rape, and the sacrifice of blood, as magical formulae. Blood and virginity have always been the most acceptable offerings to all the gods, but especially the Christian God. In the last paragraph, the reason of this is explained; it is because such sacrifices come under the Great Law of the Rosy Cross, the giving-up of the individuality, as has been explained as nauseam in previous chapters. We shall frequently recur to this subject. By "the wheel spinning in the spire" is meant the manifestation of magical force, the spermatozoon in the conical phallus. For wheels, see Chapter 78.

Commentaries.

LXIV

The Mass of the Pheonix

THIS IS THE SPECIAL NUMBER of Horus; it is the Hebrew blood, and the multiplication of the 4 by the 11, the number of Magick, explains 4 in its finest sense. But see in particular the accounts in *Equinox I*, vii of the circumstances of the Equinox of the Gods. The word "Phoenix" may be taken as including the idea of "Pelican", the bird, which is fabled to feeds its young from the blood of its own breast. Yet the two ideas, though cognate, are not identical, and "Phoenix" is the more accurate symbol. This chapter is explained in Chapter 62. It would be improper to comment further upon a ritual which has been accepted as official by the A∴ A∴.

Commentaries.

XLV

Chinese Music

THE TITLE OF THIS CHAPTER is drawn from paragraph 7. We now, for the first time, attack the question of doubt. "The Soldier and the Hunchback" should be carefully studied in this connection. The attitude recommended is scepticism, but a scepticism under control. Doubt inhibits action, as much as faith binds it. All the best Popes have been Atheists, but perhaps the greatest of them once remarked, *"Quantum nobis prodest haec fabula Christi"*. The ruler asserts facts as they are; the slave has therefore no option but to deny them passionately, in order to express his discontent. Hence such absurdities as *"Liberte, Egalite, Fraternite"*, *"In God we trust"*, and the like. The Master (in technical language, the Magus) does not concern himself with facts; he does not care whether a thing is true or not: he uses truth and falsehood in- discriminately, to serve his ends. In paragraphs 7 and 8 we find a most important statement, a practical aspect of the fact that all truth is relative, and in the last paragraph we see how scepticism keeps the mind fresh, whereas faith dies in the very sleep that it induces.

Commentaries.

XLVI

Buttons and Rosettes

THE TITLE OF THIS CHAPTER is best explained by a reference to Mistinguette and Mayol. It would be hard to decide, and it is fortunately un- necessary even to discuss, whether the distinction of their art is the cause, result, or concomitant of their private peculiarities. The fact remains that in vice, as in everything else, some things satiate, others refresh. Any game in which perfection is easily attained soon ceases to amuse, although in the beginning its fascination is so violent. Witness the tremendous, but transitory, vogue of ping-pong and diabolo. Those games in which perfection is impossible never cease to attract. The lesson of the chapter is thus always to rise hungry from a meal, always to violate one's own nature. Keep on acquiring a taste for what is naturally repugnant; this is an unfailing source of pleasure, and it has a real further advantage, in destroying the Sankharas, which, however "good" in themselves, relatively to other Sankharas, are yet barriers upon the Path; they are modifications of the Ego, and therefore those things which bar it from the absolute.

Commentaries.

XLVII

Windmill-words

THE ALLUSION IN THE TITLE is not quite clear, though it may be connected with the penultimate paragraph. The chapter consists of two points of view from which to regard Yoga, two odes upon a distant prospect of the Temple of Madura, two Elegies on a mat of Kusha-grass. The penultimate paragraph is introduced by way of repose. Cynicism is a great cure for over-study. There is a great deal of cynicism in this book, in one place and another. It should be regarded as Angostura Bitters, to brighten the flavour of a discourse which were else too sweet. It prevents one from slopping over into sentimentality

Commentaries.

XLVIII

Mome Raths

THIS CHAPTER IS PERFECTLY SIMPLE, and needs no comment whatsoever.

Commentaries.

XLIX

Wartatah-Blossoms

49 IS THE SQUARE OF 7. 7 is the passive and feminine number. The chapter should be read in connection with Chapter 31 for IT now reappears. The chapter heading, the Waratah, is a voluptuous scarlet flower, common in Australia, and this connects the chapter with Chapters 28 and 29; but this is only an allusion, for the subject of the chapter is OUR LADY BABALON, who is conceived as the feminine counterpart of IT. This does not agree very well with the common or orthodox theogony of Chapter 11; but it is to be explained by the dithyrambic nature of the chapter. In paragraph 3 NO MAN is of course NEMO, the Master of the Temple, Liber 418 will explain most of the allusions in this chapter. In paragraphs 5 and 6 the author frankly identifies him- self with the BEAST referred to in the book, and in the Apocalypse, and in LIBER LEGIS. In paragraph 6 the word "angel" may refer to his mission, and the word "lion-serpent" to the sigil of his ascending decan. (Teth= Snake=spermatozoon and Leo in the Zodiac, which like Teth itself has the snake-form. theta first written ☉ = Lingam- Yoni and Sol.) Paragraph 7 explains the theological difficulty referred to above. There is only one symbol, but

Commentaries.

this symbol has many names: of those names BABALON is the holiest. It is the name referred to in Liber Legis, 1, 22. It will be noticed that the figure, or sigil, of BABALON is a seal upon a ring, and this ring is upon the forefinger of IT. This identifies further the symbol with itself. It will be noticed that this seal, except for the absence of a border, is the official seal of the A∴ A∴. Compare Chapter 3. It is also said to be the seal upon the tombs of them that she hath slain, that is, of the Masters of the Temple. In connection with the number 49, see Liber 418, the 22nd Aethyr, as well as the usual authorities.

Commentaries.

L

The Vigil of St. Hubert

ST. HUBERT APPEARS to have been a saint who saw a stag of a mystical or sacred nature. The Stag-beetle must not be identified with the one in Chapter 16. It is a merely literary touch. The chapter is a resolution of the universe into Tetragrammaton; God the macrocosm and the microcosm beetle. Both imagine themselves to exist; both say "you" and "I", and discuss their relative reality. The things which really exist, the things which have no Ego, and speak only in the third person, regard these as ignorant, on account of their assumption of Knowledge.

Commentaries.

LI

Terrier-work

THE NUMBER 51 MEANS FAILURE AND PAIN, and its subject is appropriately doubt. The title of the chapter is borrowed from the terrible and fascinating sport of fox-hunting, which Frater Perdurabo followed in his youth. This chapter should be read in connection with "The Soldier and the Hunchback" of which it is in some sort an epitome. Its meaning is sufficiently clear, but in paragraphs 6 and 7 it will be noticed that the identification of the Soldier with the Hunchback has reached such a pitch that the symbols are interchanged, enthusiasm being represented as the sinuous snake, scepticism as the Goat of the Sabbath. In other words, a state is reached in which destruction is as much joy as creation. (Compare Chapter 46.) Beyond that is a still deeper state of mind, which is THAT.

Commentaries.

LII

The Bull-baiting

52 IS *BN*, THE NUMBER OF THE SON, Osiris-Apis, the Redeemer, with whom the Master (Fra. P.) identifies himself. he permits himself for a moment the pleasure of feeling his wounds; and, turning upon his generation, gores it with his horns. The fourscore-and-eleven books do not, we think, refer to the ninety-one chapters of this little master-piece, or even to the numerous volumes he has penned, but rather to the fact that 91 is the number of Amen, implying the completeness of his work. In the last paragraph is a paranomasia. "To chew the red rag" is a phrase for to talk aimlessly and persistently, while it is notorious that a red cloth will excite the rage of a bull.

Commentaries.

LIII

The Dowser

A DOWSER IS ONE who practises divination, usually with the object of finding water or minerals, by means of the vibrations of a hazel twig. The meadow represents the flower of life; the orchard its fruit. The paddock, being reserved for animals, represents life itself. That is to say, the secret spring of life is found in the place of life, with the result that the horse, who represents ordinary animal life, becomes the divine horse Pegasus. In paragraph 6 we see this spring identified with the phallus, for it is not only a source of water, but highly elastic, while the reference to the seasons alludes to the well-known lines of the late Lord Tennyson: "In the spring a livelier iris changes on the burnished dove, In the Spring a young man's fancy lightly turns to thoughts of love." (Locksley Hall). In paragraph 7 the place of life, the universe of animal souls, is identified with the toad, which "Ugly and venomous, Wears yet a precious jewel in his head" (Romeo and Juliet), this jewel being the divine spark in man, and indeed in all that "lives and moves and has its being". Note this phrase, which is highly significant; the word "lives" excluding the mineral kingdom, the word "moves" the vegetable kingdom, and the phrase

Commentaries.

"has its being" the lower animals, including woman. This "toad" and "jewel" are further identified with the Lotus and jewel of the well-known Buddhist phrase and this seems to suggest that this "toad" is the Yoni; the suggestion is further strengthened by the concluding phrase in brackets, "Keep us from evil", since, although it is the place of life, the means of grace, it may be ruinous.

Commentaries.

LIV

Eaves-Droppings

THE TITLE OF THIS CHAPTER refers to the duty of the Tyler in a blue lodge of Freemasons. The numbers in paragraphs 1 to 3 are significant; each Master-Mason is attended by 5 Fellow-Crafts, and each Fellow-Craft by 3 Apprentices, as if the Masters were sitting in pentagrams, and the Fellow-Craftsmen in triangles. This may refer to the number of manual signs in each of these degrees. The moral of the chapter is apparently that the mother-letter א is an inadequate solution of the Great Problem. א is identified with the Yoni, for all the symbols connected with it in this place are feminine, but א is also a number of Samadhi and mysticism, and the doctrine is therefore that Magick, in that highest sense explained in the Book of the Law, is the truer key.

Commentaries.

LV

The Drooping Sunflower

THE NUMBER 55 REFERS TO MALKUTH, the ride; it should then be read in connection with Chapters 28, 29, 49. The "drooping sunflower" is the heart, which needs the divine light. Since Jivatma was separated from Paramatma, as in paragraph 2, not only is the Divine Unity destroyed but Daath, instead of being the Child of Chokmah and Binah, becomes the Abyss, and the Qliphoth arise. The only sense which abides is that of loss, and the craving to retrieve it. In paragraph 3 it is seen that this is impossible, owing (paragraph 4) to his not having made proper arrangements to recover the original position previous to making the divisions. In paragraph 5 it is shown that this is because of allowing enjoyment to cause forgetfulness of the really important thing. Those who allow themselves to wallow in Samadhi are sorry for it afterwards. The last paragraph indicated the precautions to be taken to avoid this. The number 90 is the last paragraph is not merely fact, but symbolism; 90 being the number of Tzaddi, the Star, looked at in its exoteric sense, as a naked woman, playing by a stream, surrounded by birds and butterflies. The pole-axe is recommended instead of the usual razor, as a more vigorous weapon. One cannot be too severe in checking any faltering in the work, any digression from the Path.

Commentaries.

LVI

Trouble With Twins

THE NUMBER OF THE CHAPTER refers to Liber Legis I, 24, for paragraph 1 refers to Nuit. The "twins" in the title are those mentioned in paragraph 5. 555 is HADIT, HAD spelt in full. 156 is BABALON. In paragraph 4 is the gist of the chapter, **Laylah** being again introduced, as in Chapters 28, 29, 49 and 55. The exoteric blasphemy, it is hinted in the last paragraph, may be an esoteric arcanum, for the Master of the Temple is interested in Malkuth, as Malkuth is in Binah; also "Malkuth is in Kether, and Kether in Malkuth"; and, to the Ipsissimus, dissolution in the body of Nuit and a visit to a brothel may be identical.

Commentaries.

LVII

The Duck-Billed Platypus

THE TITLE OF THE CHAPTER suggest the two in one, since the ornithorhynchus is both bird and beast; it is also an Australian animal, like Laylah herself, and was doubtless chosen for this reason. This chapter is an apology for the universe. Paragraphs 1-3 repeat the familiar arguments against reason in an epigrammatic form. Paragraph 4 alludes to Liber Legis I, 52; "place" implies space; denies homogeneity to space; but when "place" is perfected by "t"—as it were, Yoni by Lingam—we get the word "placet", meaning "it pleases". Paragraphs 6 and 7 explain this further; it is necessary to separate things, in order that they might rejoice in uniting. See Liber Legis I, 28-30, which is paraphrased in the penultimate paragraph. In the last paragraph this doctrine is interpreted in common life by a paraphrase of the familiar and beautiful proverb, "Absence makes the heart grow fonder". (PS. I seem to get a subtle aftertaste of bitterness.) (It is to be observed that the philosopher having first committed the syllogistic error *quaternis terminorum*, in attempting to reduce the terms to three, staggers into *non distributia medii*. It is possible that considerations with Sir Wm. Hamilton's qualification (or

Commentaries.

quantification?) of the predicate may be taken as intervening, but to do so would render the humour of the chapter too subtle for the average reader in Oshkosh for whom this book is evidently written.)

Commentaries.

LVIII

Haggai-Howlings

HAGGAI, A NOTORIOUS HEBREW PROPHET, is a Second Officer in a Chapter of the Royal Arch Masons. In this chapter the author, in a sort of raging eloquence, bewails his impotence to express himself, or to induce others to follow into the light. In paragraph 1 he explains the sardonic laughter, for which he is justly celebrated, as being in reality the expression of this feeling. Paragraph 2 is a reference to the Obligation of an Entered Apprentice Mason. Paragraph 3 refers to the Ceremony of Exaltation in Royal Arch Masonry. The Initiate will be able to discover the most formidable secret of that degree concealed in the paragraph. Paragraphs 4-6 express an anguish to which that of Gethsemane and Golgotha must appear like whitlows. In paragraph 7 the agony is broken up by the sardonic or cynical laughter to which we have previously alluded. And the final paragraph, in the words of the noblest simplicity, praises the Great Work; rejoices in its sublimity, in the supreme Art, in the intensity of the passion and ecstasy which it brings forth. (Note that the words "passion" and "ecstasy" may be taken as symbolical of Yoni and Lingam.)

Commentaries.

LIX

The Tailless Monkey

The title is a euphemism for homo sapiens. The crab and the lobster are higher types of crustacae than the crayfish. The chapter is a short essay in poetic form on Determinism. It hymns the great law of Equilibrium and Compensation, but cynically criticises all philosophers, hinting that their view of the universe depends on their own circumstances. The sufferer from toothache does not agree with Doctor Pangloss, that "all is for the best in the best of all possible worlds". Nor does the wealthiest of our Dukes complain to his cronies that "Times is cruel 'ard".

Commentaries.

LX

The Wound of Amfortas

THE TITLE IS EXPLAINED IN THE NOTE. The number of the chapter may refer to the letter Samech (ס), Temperence, in the Tarot. In paragraph 1 the real chastity of Percivale or Parsifal, a chastity which did not prevent his dipping the point of the sacred lance into the Holy Grail, is distinguished from its misinterpretation by modern crapulence. The priests of the gods were carefully chosen, and carefully trained to fulfill the sacrament of fatherhood; the shame of sex consists in the usurpation of its function by the unworthy. Sex is a sacrament. The word *virtus* means "the quality of manhood". Modern "virtue" is the negation of all such qualities. In paragraph 3, however, we see the penalty of conservatism; children must be weaned. In the penultimate paragraph the words "the new Christ" alluded to the author. In the last paragraph we reach the sublime mystic doctrine that whatever you have must be abandoned. Obviously, that which differentiates your consciousness from the absolute is part of the content of that consciousness.

Commentaries.

LXI

The Fool's Knot

THE NUMBER OF THIS CHAPTER refers to the Hebrew word Ain, the negative and Ani, 61. The "fool" is the Fool of the Tarot, whose number is 0, but refers the the letter Aleph, 1. A fool's knot is a kind of knot which, although it has the appearance of a knot, is not really a knot, but pulls out immediately. The chapter consists of a series of complicated puns on 1 and I, with regard to their shape, sound, and that of the figures which resemble them in shape. Paragraph 1 calls upon the Fool of the Tarot, who is to be referred to *Ipsiss imus*, to the pure fool, Parsifal, to resolve this problem. The word Naughty suggests not only that the problem is sexual, but does not really exist. Paragraph 2 shows the Lingam and Yoni as, in conjunction, the foundation of ecstasy (I)!), and of the complete symbol I A O. The latter sentence of the paragraph unites the two meanings of giving up the Lingam to the Yoni, and the Ego to the Absolute. This idea, "I must give up", I owe, is naturally completed by I pay, and the sound of the word "pay" suggest the Hebrew letter Pe (see Liber XVI), which represents the final dissolution in Shivadarshana. In Hebrew, the letter which follows O is P; it therefore follows Ayin,

Commentaries.

the Devil of the Tarot. AYIN is spelt O I N, thus replacing the A in A I N by an O, the letter of the Devil, or Pan, the phallic God. Now AIN means nothing, and thus the replacing of AIN by OIN means the completion of the Yoni by the Lingam, which is followed by the complete dissolution symbolised in the letter P. These letters, O P, are then seen to be the root of opus, the Latin word for "work", in this case, the Great Work. And they also begin the word "opening". In Hindu philosophy, it is said that Shiva, the Destroyer, is asleep, and that when he opens his eye the universe is destroyed—another synonym, therefore, for the accomplishment of the Great Work. But the "eye" of Shiva is also his Lingam. Shiva is himself the Mahalingam, which unites these symbolisms. The opening of the eye, the ejaculation of the lingam, the destruction of the universe, the accomplishment of the Great Work—all these are different ways of saying the same thing. The last paragraph is even obscurer to those unfamiliar to the masterpiece referred to in the note; for the eye of Horus (see 777, Col. XXI, line 10, "the blind eye that weeps" is a poetic Arab name for the lingam). The doctrine is that the Great Work should be accomplished without creating new Karma, for the letter N, the fish, the vesica, the womb, breeds, whereas the Ey e of Horus does not; or, if it does so, breeds, according to Turkish tradition, a Messiah. Death implies resurrection; the

Commentaries.

illusion is reborn, as the Scythe of Death in the Tarot has a crosspiece. This is in connection with the Hindu doctrine, expressed in their injunction, "Fry your seeds". Act so as to balance your past Karma, and create no new, so that, as it were, the books are balanced. While you have either a credit or a debit, you are still in account with the universe. (N.B. Frater P. wrote this chapter—61—while dining with friends, in about a minute and a half. That is how you must know the Qabalah.)

Commentaries.

LXII

Twig?

THIS CHAPTER IS ITSELF a comment on Chapter 44.

Commentaries.

LXIII

Margery Daw

THIS CHAPTER RETURNS to the subject of **Laylah**, and to the subject already discussed in Chapters 3 and others, particularly Chapter 56. The title of the chapter refers to the old rime: "See-saw, Margery Daw, Sold her bed to lie upon straw. Was not she a silly slut, To sell her bed to lie upon dirt?" The word "see-saw" is significant, almost a comment upon this chapter. To the Master of the Temple opposite rules apply. His unity seeks the many, and the many is again transmuted to the one. *Solve et Coagula.*

Commentaries.

LXIV

Constancy

64 IS THE NUMBER OF MERCURY, and of the intelligence of that planet, Din and Doni. The moral of the chapter is that one wants liberty, although one may not wish to exercise it: the author would readily die in defence of the right of Englishmen to play football, or of his own right not to play it. (As a great poet has expressed it: "We don't want to fight, but, by Jingo, if we do-") This is his meaning towards his attitude to complete freedom of speech and action. He refuses to listen to the ostensible criticism of the spirits, and explains his own position. Their real mission was to rouse him to confidence and action.

Commentaries.

LXV

Sic Transeat —

65 IS THE NUMBER OF ADONAI, the Holy Guardian Angel; see Liber 65, Liber Konx Om Pax, and other works of reference. The chapter title means, "So may he pass away", the blank obviously referring to N E M O. The "moonpool of silver" is the Path of Gimel, leading from Tiphareth to Kether; the "flames of violet" are the Ajna-Chakkra; the lily itself is Kether, the lotus of the Sahasrara. "Lily" is spelt with a capital to connect with Laylah.

Commentaries.

LXVI

The Praying Mantis

66 IS THE NUMBER OF ALLAH; the praying mantis is a blasphemous grasshopper which caricatures the pious. The chapter recurs to the subject of **Laylah**, whom the author exalts above God, in continuation of the reasonings given in Chapter 56 and 63. She is identified with N.O.X. by the quotation from Liber 65.

Commentaries.

LXVII

Sodom-apples

THIS CHAPTER MEANS THAT it is useless to try to abandon the Great Work. You may occupy yourself for a time with other things, but you will only increase your bitterness, rivet the chains still on your feet. Paragraph 4 is a practical counsel to mystics not to break up their dryness by relaxing their austerities. The last paragraph will only be understood by Masters of the Temple.

Commentaries.

LXVIII

Manna

MANNA WAS A HEAVENLY CAKE which, in the legend, fed the Children of Israel in the Wilderness. The author laments the failure of his mission to mankind, but comforts himself with the following reflections: (1) He enjoys the advantages of solitude. (2) Previous prophets encountered similar difficulties in convincing their hearers. (3) Their food was not equal to that obtainable at Rumpelmayer's. (4) In a few days I am going to rejoin Laylah. (5) My mission will succeed soon enough. (6) Death will remove the nuisance of success.

Commentaries.

LXIX

The Way to Succeed-And the Way to Suck Eggs!

THE KEY TO THE UNDERSTANDING of this chapter is given in the number and the title, the former being intelligible to all nations who employ Arabic figures, the latter only to experts in deciphering English puns. The chapter alludes to Levi's drawing of the Hexagram, and is a criticism of, or improvement upon, it. In the ordinary Hexagram, the Hexagram of nature, the red triangle is upwards, like fire, and the blue triangle downwards, like water. In the magical hexa- gram this is revered; the descending red triangle is that of Horus, a sign specially revealed by him personally, at the Equinox of the Gods. (It is the flame desending upon the altar, and licking up the burnt offering.) The blue triangle represents the aspiration, since blue is the colour of devotion, and the triangle, kinetically considered, is the symbol of directed force. In the first three paragraphs this formation of the hexagram is explained; it is a symbol of the mutual separation of the Holy Guardian Angel and his client. In the interlocking is indicated the completion of the work. Paragraph 4 explains in slightly different language what we have said above, and the

Commentaries.

scriptural image of tongues is introduced. In paragraph 5 the symbolism of tongues is further developed. Abrahadabra is our primal example of an interlocked word. We assume that the reader has thoroughly studied that word in Liber D., etc. The sigil of Cancer links up this symbolism with the number of the chapter. The remaining paragraphs continue the Gallic symbolism.

Commentaries.

LXX

Broomstick-babblings

70 IS THE NUMBER of the letter Ain, the Devil in the Tarot. The chapter refers to the Witches' Sabbath, the description of which in Payne Knight should be carefully read before studying this chapter. All the allusions will then be obvious, save those which we proceed to not. Sanhedrim, a body of 70 men. An Eye. Eye in Hebrew is Oin, 70. The "gnarled oak" and the "glacier torrent" refer to the confessions made by many witches. I paragraph 7 is seen the meaning of the chapter; the obscene and distorted character of much of the universe is a whim of the Creator.

Commentaries.

LXXI

King's College Chapel

THIS CHAPTER IS A PLAIN statement of fact, put in anthem form for emphasis. The title is due to the circumstances of the early piety of Frater Perdurabo, who was frequently refreshed by hearing the anthems in this chief of the architectural glories of his Alma Mater.

Commentaries.

LXXII

Hashed Pheasant

THERE ARE THREE CONSECUTIVE VERSES in the Pentateuch, each containing 72 letters. If these be written beneath each other, the middle verse bring reversed, i.e. as in English, and divisions are then made vertically, 72 tri-lateral names are formed, the sum of which is Tetragrammaton; this is the great and mysterious Divided Name; by adding the terminations Yod He, or Aleph Lamed, the names of 72 Angels are formed. The Hebrews say that by uttering this Name the universe is destroyed. This statement means the same as that of the Hindus, that the effective utterance of the name of Shiva would cause him to awake, and so destroy the universe. In Egyptian and Gnostic magick we meet with pylons and Aeons, which only open on the utterance of the proper word. In Mohammedan magick we find a similar doctrine and practice; and the whole of Mantra-Yoga has been built on this foundation. Thoth, the god of Magick, is the inventor of speech; Christ is the Logos. Lines 1-4 are now clear. In lines 507 we see the results of Shivadarshana. Do not imagine that any single ides, however high, however holy (or even however insignificant!!), can escape the destruction. The logician my say, "But white

Commentaries.

exists, and if white is destroyed, it leaves black; yet black exists. So that in that case at least one known phenomenon of this universe is identical with one of that." Vain word! The logician and his logic are alike involved in the universal ruin. Lines 8-11 indicate that this fact is the essential one about Shivadarshana. The title is explained by the intentionally blasphemous puns and colloquialisms of lines 9 and 10.

Commentaries.

VXXIII

The Devil, the Ostrich, and the Orphan Child

THE HEBREW LETTER GIMEL adds up to 73; it means a camel. The title of the chapter is borrowed from the well-known lines of Rudyard Kipling: "But the commissariat camel, when all is said and done, 'E's a devil and an awstridge and an orphan-child in one." Paragraph 1 may imply a dogma of death as the highest form of initiation. Initiation is not a simple phenomenon. Any given initiation must take place on several planes, and is not always conferred on all of these simultaneously. Intellectual and moral perception of truth often, one might almost say usually, precedes spiritual and physical perceptions. One would be foolish to claim initiation unless it were complete on every plane. Paragraph 2 will easily be understood by those who have practised Asana. there is perhaps a sardonic reference to rigor mortis, and certainly one conceives the half-humorous attitude of the expert towards the beginner. Paragraph 3 is a comment in the same tone of rough good nature. The word Zelator is used because the Zelator of the A∴ A∴ has to pass an examination in Asana before he becomes eligible for the grade of Practicus. The ten days allude merely to the tradition about the camel, that he can go ten days

Commentaries.

without water. Paragraph 4 identifies the reward of initiation with death; it is a cessation of all that we call life, in a way in which what we call death is not. 3, silver, and the moon, are all correspondences of Gimel, the letter of the Aspiration, since gimel is the Path that leads from the Microcosm in tiphareth to the Macrocosm in Kether. The epithets are far too complex to explain in detail, but Mem, the Hanged man, has a close affinity for Gimel, as will be seen by a study of Liber 418. Unt is not only the Hindustani for Camel, but the usual termination of the third person plural of the present tense of Latin words of the Third and Fourth Conjugations. The reason for thus addresing the reader is that he has now transcended the first and second persons. Cf. Liber LXV, Chapter III, vv. 21-24, and FitzGerald's Omar Khayyam: "Some talk there was of Thee and Me There seemed; and then no more of Thee and Me.") The third person plural must be used, because he has now perceived himself to be a bundle of impressions. For this is the point on the Path of Gimel when he is actually crossing the Abyss; the student must consult the account of this given in "The Temple of Solomon the King". The Ego is but "the ghost of a non-Ego", the imaginary focus at which the non-Ego becomes sensible. Paragraph 5 expresses the wish of the Guru that his Chela may attain safely to binah, the Mother. Paragraph 6 whispers the ultimate and dread secret of initiation into his ear, identifying the

Commentaries.

vastness of the Most Holy with the obscene worm that gnaws the bowels of the damned.

Commentaries.

LXXIV

Carey Street

Carey Street is well known to poor Englishmen as the seat of the Bankruptcy buildings. Paragraphs 1-4 are in prose, the downward course, and the rest of the chapter in poetry, the upward. The first part shows the fall from Nought in four steps; the second part, the return. The details of this Hierarchy have already been indicated in various chapters. It is quite conventional mysticism. Step 1, the illumination of Ain as Ain Soph Aour; step 2, the concentration of Ain Soph Aour in Kether; step 3, duality and the rest of it down to Malkuth; step 4, the stooping of Malkuth to the Qliphoth, and the consequent ruin of the Tree of Life. Part 2 show the impossibility of stopping on the Path of Adeptship. The final couplet represents the first step upon the Path, which must be taken even although the aspirant is intellectually aware of the severity of the whole course. You must give up the world for love, the material for the moral idea, before that, in its turn, is surrendered to the spiritual. And so on. This is a **Laylah**-chapter, but in it **Laylah** figures as the mere woman.

Commentaries.

LXXV

Plovers' Eggs

THE TITLE IS EXPLAINED IN THE NOTE, but also alludes to paragraph 1, the plover's egg being often contemporary with the early strawberry. Paragraph 1 means that change of diet is pleasant; vanity pleases the mind; the idee fixe is a sign of insanity. See paragraphs 4 and 5. Paragraph 6 puts the question, "Then is sanity or insanity desirable?" The oak is weakened by the ivy which clings around it, but perhaps the ivy keeps it from going mad. The next paragraph expresses the difficulty of expressing thought in writing; it seems, on the face of it, absurd that the the text of this book, composed as it is of English, simple, austere, and terse, should need a commentary. But it does so, or my most gifted Chela and myself would hardly have been at the pains to write one. It was in response to the impassioned appeals of many most worthy brethren that we have yielded up that time and thought which gold could not have bought, or torture wrested. Laylah is again the mere woman.

Commentaries.

LXVI

Phaeton

PHAETON WAS THE CHARIOTEER of the Sun in Greek mythology. At first sight the prose of this chapter, though there is only one dissyllable in it, appears difficult; but this is a glamour cast by Maya. It is a compendium of various systems of philosophy. No = Nihilism; Yes = Monism, and all dogmatic systems; Perhaps = Pyrrhonism and Agnosticism; O! = The system of Liber Legis. (See Chapter 0.) Eye = Phallicism (cf. Chapters 61 and 70); I = Fichteanism; Hi! = Transcendentalism; Y? = Scepticism, and the method of science. No denies all these and closes the argument. But all this is a glamour cast by Maya; the real meaning of the prose of this chapter is as follows: No, some negative conception beyond the IT spoken of in Chapters 31, 49 and elsewhere. Yes, IT. Perhaps, the flux of these. O!, Nuit, Hadit, Ra-Hoor-Khuit. Eye, the phallus in Kether. I, the Ego in Chokmah. Hi!, Binah, the feminine principle fertilised. (He by Yod.) Y?, the Abyss. No, the refusal to be content with any of this. But all this is again only a glamour of Maya, as previously observed in the text (Chapter 31). All this is true and false, and it is true and false to say that it is true and false. The prose of this chapter combines, and of course denies, all these meanings, both

Commentaries.

singly and in combination. It is intended to stimulate thought to the point where it explodes with violence and forever. A study of this chapter is probably the best short cut to Nibbana. The thought of the Master in this chapter is exceptionally lofty. That this is the true meaning, or rather use, of this chapter, is evident from the poetry. The master salutes the previous paragraphs as horses which, although in themselves worthless animals (without the epithets), carry the Charioteer in th e path of the Sun. The question, How? Not by their own virtues, but by the silence which results when they are all done with. The word "neigh" is a pun on "nay", which refers to the negative conception already postulated as beyond IT. The suggestion is, that there may be something falsely described as silence, to represent absence-of-conception beyond that negative. It would be possible to interpret this chapter in its entirety as an adverse criticism of metaphysics as such, and this is doubtless one of its many submeanings.

Commentaries.

LXXVII

The Sublime and Supreme Septenary in its Mature Magical Manifestation through Matter : As it is Written : An He-goat also

77 IS THE NUMBER OF Laylah (LAILAH), to whom this chapter is wholly devoted. The first section of the title is an analysis of 77 considered as a mystic number. 7, the septenary; 11, the magical number; 77, the mani- festation, therefore, of the septenary. Through matter, because 77 is written in Hebrew Ayin Zayin (OZ), and He-Goat, the symbol of matter, Capricornus, the Devil of the Tarot; which is the picture of the Goat of the Sabbath upon an altar, worshipped by two other devils, male and female. As will be seen from the photogravure inserted opposite this chapter, Laylah is herself not devoid of "Devil", but, as she habitually remarks, on being addressed in terms implying this fact, "It's nice to be a devil when you're one like me." The text need no comment, but it will be noticed that it is much shorter that the title. Now, the Devil of the Tarot is the Phallus, the Redeemer, and Laylah symbolises redemption to Frater P. The number 77, also, interpreted as in the title, is the redeeming force. The ratio of the length of title and text is the key to the true meaning of the chapter, which is, that Redemption is really

Commentaries.

as simple as it appears complex, that the names (or veils) of truth are obscure and many, the Truth itself plain and one; but that the latter must be reached through the former. This chapter is therefore an apology, were one needed, for the Book of Lies itself. In these few simple words, it explains the necessity of the book, and offers it- humbly, yet with confidence-as a means of redemption to the world of sorrowing men. The name with full-stops: L.A.Y.L.A.H. represents an analysis of the name, which may be left to the ingenium of the advanced practicus.

Commentaries.

LXXVIII

Wheel and — Woa!

THE NUMBER OF THIS CHAPTER is that of the cards of the Tarot. The title of this chapter is a pun of the phrase "weal and woe". It means motion and rest. The moral is the conventional mystic one; stop thought at its source! Five wheels are mentioned in this chapter; all but the third refer to the universe as it is; but the wheel of the Tarot is not only this, but represents equally the Magickal Path. This practice is therefore given by Frater P. to his pupils; to treat the sequence of the cards as cause and effect. Thence, to discover the cause behind all causes. Success in this practice qualifies for the grade of Master of the Temple. In the penultimate paragraph the bracketed passage reminds the student that the universe is not to be contemplated as a phenomenon in time.

Commentaries.

LXXIX

The Bal Bullier

THE TITLE OF THIS CHAPTER is a place frequented by Frater P. until it became respectable. The chapter is a rebuke to those who can see nothing but sorrow and evil in the universe. The Buddhist analysis may be true, but not for men of courage. The plea that "love is sorrow", because its ecstasies are only transitory, is contemptible. Paragraph 5. Coote is a blackmailer exposed by *The Equinox*. The end of the paragraph refers to Catullus, his famous epigram about the youth who turned his uncle into Harpocrates. It is a subtle way for Frater P. to insist upon his virility, since otherwise he could not employ the remedy. The last paragraph is a quotation. The word "Sadist" is taken from the famous Marquis de Sade, who gave supreme literary form to the joys of torture.

Commentaries.

LXXX

Blackthorn

FRATER P. CONTINUES THE SUBJECT of Chapter 79. He pictures himself as a vigorous, reckless, almost rowdy Irishman. he is no thin-lipped prude, to seek salvation in unmanly self-abnegation; no Creeping Jesus, to slink through existence to the tune of the Dead March in Saul; no Cremerian Callus to warehouse his semen in his cerebellum. "New Thoughtist" is only Old Eunuch writ small. Paragraph 2 gives the very struggle for life, which disheartens modern thinkers, as a good enough reason for existence. Paragraph 5 expresses the sorrow of the modern thinker, and paragraph 6 Frater P.'s suggestion for replying to such critics.

Commentaries.

LXXXI

Louis Lingg

THE TITLE IS THE NAME of one of the authors of the affair of the Haymarket, in Chicago. See Frank Harris, "The Bomb". Paragraph 1 explains that Frater P. sees no use in the employment of such feeble implements as bombs. Nor does he agree even with the aim of the Anarchists, since, although Anarchists themselves need no restraint, not daring to drink cocoa, lest their animal passions should be aroused (as Olivia Haddon assures my favourite Chela), yet policemen, unless most severely repressed, would be dangerous wild beasts. The last bitter sentence is terribly true; the personal liberty of the Russian is immensely greater than that of the Englishman. The latest Radical devices for securing freedom have turned nine out of ten Englishmen into Slaves, obliged to report their movements to the government like so many ticket-of-leave men.

Commentaries.

LXXXII

Bortsch

THE TITLE OF THIS CHAPTER, and its two subtitles, will need no explanation to readers of the classics. This poem, inspired by Jane Cheron, is as simple as it is elegant. The poet asks, in verse 1, How can we baffle the Three Characteristics? In verse 2, he shows that death is impotent against life. In verse 3, he offers the solution of the problem. This is, to accept things as they are, and to turn your whole energies to progress on the Path.

Commentaries.

LXXXIII

The Blind Pig

THE TITLE OF THIS CHAPTER refers to the Greek number, PG being "Pig" without an "i". The subject of the chapter is consequently corollary to Chapters 79 and 80, the ethics of Adept life. The Adept has performed the Great Work; He has reduced the Many to Naught; as a consequence, he is no longer afraid of the Many. Paragraph 4. See berashith. Paragraph 5, takes things for what they are; give up interpreting, refining away, analysing. Be simple and lucid and radiant as Frater P. Paragraph 6. With this commentary there is no further danger, and the warning becomes superfluous.

Commentaries.

LXXXIV

The Avalanche

THIS CONTINUES THE SUBJECT of Chapter 83. The title refers to the mental attitude of the Master; the avalanche does not fall because it is tired of staying on the mountain, or in order to crush the Alps below it, or because that it feels that it needs exercise. Perfectly unconscious, perfectly indifferent, it obeys the laws of Cohesion and of Gravitation. It is the sun and its own weight that loosen it. So, also, is the act of the Adept. "Delivered from the lust of result, he is every way perfect." Paragraphs 1 and 2. By "devotion to Frater Perdurabo" is not meant sycophancy, but intelligent reference and imaginative sympathy. Put your mind in tune with his; identify yourself with him as he seeks to identify himself with the Intelligence that communicates to him the Holy Books. Paragraphs 3 and 4 are explained by the 13th Aethyr and the title.

Commentaries.

LXXXV

Borborygmi

WE NOW RETURN to that series of chapters which started with Chapter 8 (H). The chapter is perfectly simple and needs no comment.

Commentaries.

LXXXVI

Tat

THE NUMBER 86 REFERS TO ELOHIM, the name of the elemental forces. The title is the Sanskrit for That, in its sense of "The Existing". This chapter is an attempt to replace Elohim by a more satisfactory hieroglyph of the elements. The best attribution of Elohim is Aleph, Air; Lamed, Earth; He, Spirit; Yod, Fire; Mem, Water. But the order is not good; Lamed is not satisfactory for Earth, and Yod too spiritualised a form of Fire. (But see Book 4, part III.) Paragraphs 1-6. Out of Nothing, Nothing is made. The word Nihil is taken to affirm that the universe is Nothing, and that is now to be analysed. The order of the element is that of Jeheshua. The elements are taken rather as in Nature; N is easily Fire, since Mars is the ruler of Scorpio: the virginity of I suits Air and Water, elements which in Magick are closely interwoven: H, the letter of of breath, is suitable for Spirit; Abrahadabra is called the name of Spirit, because it is cheth: L is Earth, green and fertile, because Venus, the greenness, fertility, and earthiness of things is the Lady of Libra, Lamed. In paragraph 7 we turn to the so-called Jetziratic attribution of Pentagrammaton, that followed by Dr. Dee, and by the Hindus,

Commentaries.

Tibetans, Chinese and Japanese. Fire is the Foundation, the central core, of things; above this forms a crust, tormented from below, and upon this condenses the original steam. Around this flows the air, created by Earth and Water through the action of vegetation. Such is the globe; but all this is a mere strain in the aethyr, Αιθηρ. Here is a new Pentagrammaton, presumably suitable for another analysis of the elements; but after a different manner. Alpha (A) is Air; Rho (P) the Sun; these are the Spirit and the Son of Christian theology. In the midst is the Father, expressed as Father-and-Mother. I-H (Yod and He), Eta (H) being used to express "the Mother" instead of Epsilon (E), to show that She has been impregnated by the Spirit; it is the rough breathing and not the soft. The centre of all is Theta (Θ), which was originally written as a point in a circle (☉), the sublime hieroglyph of the Sun in the Macrocosm, and in the Microcosm of the Lingam in conjunction with the Yoni. This word Αιθηρ (Aethyr) is therefore a perfect hieroglyph of the Cosmos in terms of Gnostic Theology. The reader should consult La Messe et ses Mysteres, par Jean 'Marie de V' (Paris et Nancy, 1844), for a complete demonstration of the incorporation of the Solar and Phallic Mysteries in Christianity.

Commentaries.

LXXXVII

Mandarin-Meals

THIS CHAPTER IS TECHNICALLY one of the **Laylah** chapters. It means that, however great may be one's own achievements, the gifts from on high are still better. The Sigil is taken from a Gnostic talisman, and refers to the Sacrament.

Commentaries.

LXXXVIII

Gold Bricks

THE TERM "GOLD BRICKS" is borrowed from American finance. The chapter is a setting of an old story. A man advertises that he could tell anyone how to make four hundred a year certain, and would do so on receipt of a shilling. To every sender he dispatched a post-card with these words: "Do as I do." The word "sucker" is borrowed from American finance. The moral of the chapter is, that it is no good trying to teach people who need to be taught.

Commentaries.

LXXXIX

Unprofessional Conduct

FRATER P. HAD BEEN ANNOYED by a scurvy doctor, the number of whose house was 89. He shows that his mind was completely poisoned in respect of that number by his allowing himself to be annoyed. (But note that a good Qabalist cannot err. "In Him all is right." 89 is Body-that which annoys-and the Angel of the Lord of Despair and Cruelty. Also "Silence" and "Shut Up". The four meanings completely describe the chapter.)

Commentaries.

XC

Starlight

THIS CHAPTER IS A SORT of final Confession of Faith. It is the unification of all symbols and all planes. The End is expressible

Commentaries.

XCI

The Heikle

THE "HEIKLE" IS TO BE DISTINGUISHED from the "Huckle", which latter is defined in the late Sir W.S. Gilbert's "Prince Cherry-Top". A clear definition of the Heikle might have been obtained from Mr Oscar Eckenstein, 34 Greencroft Gardens, South Hampstead, London, N.W. (when this comment was written). But its general nature is that of a certain minute whiteness, appearing at the extreme end of great blackness. It is a good title for the last chapter of this book, and it also symbolises the eventual coming out into the light of his that has wandered long in the darkness. 91 is the numeration of Amen. The chapter consists of an analysis of this word, but gives no indication as to the result of this analysis, as if to imply this: The final Mystery is always insoluble.

FINIS. CORONAT OPUS.

Jabberwoke Pocket Occult Collection

CRYSTAL GAZING by Frater Achad

Thus, it is hoped, all will be satisfied; and should their satisfaction be equal to that of the Author at this opportunity to herald the Light – however faintly – of the Ultimate Crystalline Sphere.

ISBN: 978-1-954873-36-0
$11.00 USD
FraterAchadCrystalGazing.com

HEAVENLY BRIDEGROOMS by Ida Craddock

"One of the most remarkable human documents ever produced... This book is of incalculable value to every student of Occult matters. No Magick library is complete without it" – A.C.

ISBN: 978-1-954873-21-6
$14.00 USD
HeavenlyBridegrooms.com

MOONCHILD by Aleister Crowley

The cattiest & messiest novel from the transcriber of the Wickedest Man in England. Hiding behind the guise of fiction, Moonchild is the Beast's platform to slander his many nemeses inside the spiritualist circles of London.

ISBN: 978-1-954873-53-7
$19.00 USD /
AleisterCrowleyMoonchild.com

THE KYBALION by Three Initiates

There is no portion of the occult teachings which have been so closely guarded as the fragments of the Hermetic Teachings, the Great Central Sun of Occultism, whose rays have illuminated the teachings promulgated since all time.

ISBN: 978-1-954873-08-7
$14.00 USD
ThreeInitiatesKybalion.com

THE SO-CALLED OCCULT by Carl Jung

A 20-year-old Carl Jung attends his cousin's seances leading to a psychological investigation of hauntings, witch-sleeps, and delicious bliss that unravels into obsession.

ISBN: 978-1-954873-39-1
$14.00 USD
TheSoCalledOccult.com

THE GREAT GOD PAN *by Arthur Machen*

A classic of pagan horror that follows the trail of destruction left in the wake of a mysterious socialite, as she serves the will of her shadowy, horned benefactor.

ISBN: 978-1-954873-35-3
$14.00 USD
AllHailPan.com

THE WITCH CULT *by Margaret Murray*

Firsthand accounts of a pre-Christian witch cult that worshiped the Horned God of fertility—whose Christian persecutors referred to him as the Devil—and the nocturnal rites performed at the witches' Sabbath.

ISBN: 978-1-954873-33-9
$19.00 USD
TheWitchCult.com

THE BOOK OF LIES *by Frater Perdurabo*

A collection of falsehoods from Dionysus, received by the mysterious Frater Perdurabo and the Scarlet Woman LAYLAH. This wicked book is said to contain within its pages the secret truth of the universe . . . readers beware.

ISBN: 978-1-954873-37-7
$14.00 USD
FaleslyCalledBreaks.com

A MIDSOMMAR NIGHT'S DREAM *by William Shakespeare*

The timeless ethereal tale of four Lovers who wander too close to the games of Titania and Oberon, the Faerie Queen and King, and their encounters with the archetypal Tickster Puck and all the fantastical beings whom inhabit the woodland realm.

ISBN: 978-1-954873-54-4
$11.00 USD
MidsommarNightsDream.com

SATAN: A NOVEL *by Mark Twain*

The greatest and final novel from the master of American fiction, Mark Twain's fable of an angelic visitation in the Austrian countryside reveals the solipsism of its author, and his belief of the unreality of our collective dream.

ISBN: 978-1-954873-59-9
$16.00 USD
MarkTwainSatan.com

JABBERWOKE © MMXXI

Wholesale Inquiries:
contact@jabberwokebooks.com

www.ingramcontent.com/pod-product-compliance
Lightning Source LLC
Chambersburg PA
CBHW021441070526
44577CB00002B/240